Praise for *No Cure for Being Human*

"I began reading *No Cure for Being Human* after dinner one evening and didn't move until I finished the last gorgeous page. As I finally put this masterpiece down, I thought: Kate Bowler is the only one we can trust to tell us the truth. Bowler is a prophet and her new offering is another true gift to the world. This book will open minds and warm hearts."
—GLENNON DOYLE, author of the
#1 *New York Times* bestseller *Untamed*

"Bowler offers an alternative to the good vibes/prosperity gospel approach: honesty with room for mystery and humor." —*The New York Times*

"This interior monologue about her cancer battle and her life is unputdownable in its blunt honesty, soulfulness, and vulnerability."
—ZIBBY OWENS, Katie Couric Media

"Kate Bowler is a truth-teller who shows us how to hold the terrible and the beautiful in one hand. *No Cure for Being Human* is a must-read for anyone whose life has been bifurcated into a before and after—which is to say all of us. In this roadmap though the messy middle, Bowler's words are a soothing balm, like a late-night conversation with a best friend. Every page shimmers with wit and wisdom."
—SULEIKA JAOUAD, author of
Between Two Kingdoms

"A gripping, raw, page-by-page account of one woman trying to make sense of the wrongness of the world in the midst of her fight with cancer. She doesn't shy away from the hard stuff and she relates to the reader, just one human to another struggling in an unjust world."
—*U.S. Catholic*

"Those in need of a wake-up call will find it in this breathtaking narrative. Bowler's strong faith is present throughout, though the writing, refreshingly, never feels overtly religious. Her convictions underscore the importance of living life on one's own terms."
—*Publishers Weekly* (starred review)

"Bowler's affecting narrative meditates on the things she's just faced; she also takes it as an opportunity to reflect on the past and the kind of life she wants for herself in the future. Bowler writes about all of it with good humor, occasional anger, and vivid honesty. . . . Through it all, she survives, offering along the way fresh insight on life and chronic illness. Readers will be engrossed by this heartfelt memoir of sickness, family, and recovery."
—*Library Journal*

"Wise, wry reflections on living in the face of uncertainty. . . . Like others who have suffered traumatic loss or illness—especially during the pandemic—Bowler recognizes that "so often the experiences that define us are the ones we didn't pick." A sensitive memoir of survival."
—*Kirkus Reviews*

"Bowler's prose is adept at capturing the dialectic of life's 'splendid, ragged edges' showing through. And she's funny, too. This is a gem for cancer patients and their families and for survivors, but really, for anyone who understands the terror and beauty of being human."   —*Booklist*

"With dry wit and unflinching honesty, Kate Bowler grapples with her diagnosis, her ambition, and her faith as she tries to come to terms with her limitations in a culture that says anything is possible."
                                                        —*Bookreporter*

"Bowler—intriguingly described as 'a Christian Joan Didion' by Glennon Doyle—is funny, extremely direct, and wise; she also survived cancer against improbable odds. *No Cure for Being Human* picks up the threads of that memoir with another aphorism as a title, though this one revels in human mess, brokenness, and crooked lines."   —*INDY Week*

"*No Cure for Being Human* is the wry, touching follow-up to Bowler's 2018 memoir, *Everything Happens for a Reason*. Here, Bowler continues to combat unhelpful religious/self-help mantras as she ponders what to do with the extra time medical breakthroughs have given her. The book's bittersweet tone finds the humor as well as the tragedy in a cancer diagnosis."
                                                    —*Shelf Awareness*

"In her new book, *No Cure for Being Human*, Bowler continues to resist easy platitudes in favor of hard-earned wisdom, sharing these truths to help readers build a faith deep and honest enough to withstand life's inevitable storms. . . . Bowler's ability to tackle dark subjects with humor draws you in. But it is her raw honesty that makes you stop, reread and reflect."

—*The Prebysterian Outlook*

"With grace, wisdom, and humor, Kate Bowler encourages us to cut back on self-help Kool-Aid and teaches what it means to be human."

—ADAM GRANT, #1 *New York Times* bestselling author of *Think Again*

"Kate Bowler has paid through the nose with terrifying realities to become a writer of uncommon spiritual wisdom, coupled with an amazing sense of humor and a heart full of love. She fills me with hope."

—ANNE LAMOTT, author of *Dusk, Night, Dawn*

"In a culture that asks us to constantly strive and improve, Kate Bowler recognizes that your own pain is neither an aberration nor an opportunity but a fact of life. There is nobody on earth who sees our humanity quite like Kate Bowler."

—NORA MCINERNY, author of *No Happy Endings* and creator and host of the podcast *Terrible, Thanks for Asking*

"I couldn't put this brilliant memoir down (and I underlined many passages). Kate Bowler is the rare author who can explore difficult subjects with both breathtaking honesty and light-heartedness. She brings profound insight and love to the human experience."

—GRETCHEN RUBIN, author of *The Happiness Project*

"Kate Bowler refuses to jump on the bandwagon of toxic positivity. Instead, she leads us to a truer truth: the work is unfinishable, and so be it. I find my interactions with the mind of Kate Bowler more useful and comforting than most all others combined."

—KELLY CORRIGAN, author and host of the podcast *Kelly Corrigan Wonders* and PBS's *Tell Me More with Kelly Corrigan*

"With hilarity and courage, Bowler tells the story of being diagnosed with stage-four cancer at age thirty-five, which forced her to re-examine the way she (and we) live our lives. This is a brilliant examination of what happens when everything you assumed is suddenly in question, and you have to substitute love for self-actualization and hope for certainty."

—LORI GOTTLIEB, author of *Maybe You Should Talk To Someone*

"I have long admired Kate. She has an amazing ability to honor heartbreak while evoking smiles."

—KRISTA TIPPETT, creator and host of the radio show and podcast *On Being*

"*No Cure For Being Human* is an amazing resource. I hope everyone whom this topic touches will remember *No Cure*."

—DAX SHEPARD, cohost of the podcast *Armchair Expert*

NO CURE FOR

BEING HUMAN

No Cure for Being Human

(AND OTHER TRUTHS
I NEED TO HEAR)

—

Kate Bowler

RANDOM HOUSE · NEW YORK

Published in the United States by Random House, an imprint and
division of Penguin Random House LLC, New York.

RANDOM HOUSE and the HOUSE colophon are registered trademarks of
Penguin Random House LLC.

Originally published in hardcover in the United States by Random
House, an imprint and division of Penguin Random House LLC, in 2021.

LIBRARY OF CONGRESS CATALOGING-IN-PUBLICATION DATA
Names: Bowler, Kate, author.
Title: No cure for being human : (and other truths I need to hear) /
Kate Bowler.
Description: New York : Random House, 2021.
Identifiers: LCCN 2021010350 (print) | LCCN 2021010351 (ebook) |
ISBN 9780593230794 (trade paperback) | ISBN 9780593230787 (ebook)
Subjects: LCSH: Bowler, Kate,—Health. | Colon (Anatomy)—Cancer—
Patients—United States—Biography. | Cancer—Patients—
Family relationships.
Classification: LCC RC280.C6 B683 2021 (print) |
LCC RC280.C6 (ebook) | DDC 616.99/43470092 [B]—dc23
LC record available at https://lccn.loc.gov/2021010350
LC ebook record available at https://lccn.loc.gov/2021010351

Printed in the United States of America on acid-free paper

randomhousebooks.com

2 4 6 8 9 7 5 3

FOR MY FLYING BUTTRESSES

CHELSEA AND KATHERINE

WHO BUILT ME FROM THE OUTSIDE IN

CONTENTS

CONTENTS

AUTHOR'S NOTE

—

ALL MEMOIRS ARE, OF COURSE, SUBJECT TO the vagaries of memory. As a historian, I try my best to meet the exacting standards of my profession. I relied heavily on my medical records, journals, and interviews to reconstruct my diagnosis and treatment with as much accuracy as possible. In order to preserve the privacy of my friends and arch-nemeses, I modified identifying details and changed the following names: Linda, Caitlin, Dr. Cartwright, Derek, Steve, Patrick, and Max.

PREFACE

—

I AM A PROFESSOR OF HISTORY, SO I KNOW THIS in my bones: nothing is inevitable. History is made by people who stared, blinking, into the uncertain future. Their paths were not lit before them by sacred meteors. For most of us, this sounds like good news. We choose and choose and choose again.

Before the baby, before the diagnosis, before the pandemic. Before. Before when I was earnest and clever and ignorant, I thought, *life is a series of choices.* I curated my own life until, one day, I couldn't. I had accepted the burden of limitless choices only to find that I had few to make. I was stuck in this body, this house, this life.

American culture has popular theories about how to build a perfect life. You can have it all if you just learn how to conquer your limits. There is infinity lurking somewhere at the bottom of your inbox or in the stack of self-help books on the bedside table. It taunts you as you grip the steering wheel in traffic, attempting your new breathing practice, or in the predawn minutes when you could be working out.

I have seen these guides to endless progress for sale in airport kiosks. Some are written by spiritual guides promising to reveal God's single plan and purpose for my life. "Trust God and the path will reveal itself." Other books call for wild action. There are oceans to plumb and mountains to climb and planes to exit midair. *Carpe diem!* Try *The 4-Hour Workweek* to escape the daily grind, or check out the latest research on eliminating distraction. There are bucket lists galore with glossy photographs of thrills and architectural wonders; calendars with rituals to eradicate inefficiencies; and writing journals juiced with visionary wisdom from gurus and titans of industry. These are the formulas for a meaningful life, how to live one and how to end one.

But the truth is somewhere inside of me: *there is no formula. We live and we are loved and we are gone.*

Tumors budded and spread across my colon and liver without my consent, and here I am. I feel a spark of horror each time I remember it: we come undone.

This is what happens to all of us. We fall ill. We get old. We can't have that baby or keep that relationship. We missed our chance to go to this school or take that job. Our parents die before we know them, and our kids forget our love. We lose people before we can learn to live without them.

I want to believe I'm independent, but I am caught in a web, and every choice I make pulls at its threads. Is this a good decision? Will this choice hold? Who else suffers if the web comes unraveled? I am not my own. At this moment, I can hear the stirring of my husband, Toban, his heavy footfall in the hallway followed by the soft hiss of the water pipes for his shower. My young son, Zach, is curled into a blanket like a puppy at my feet, his blond head catching the sideways light of the morning. The computer monitor is casting a poor reflection of this room, its stacks of dog-eared books and walls lined from floor to ceiling with my sister's framed watercolors: my husband and me as teenagers; my father hugging me at the world's largest Noah's Ark; me, like a benevolent zookeeper, cradling Zach in his teddy-bear sleeper. I look around me and I think, *these are the choices I've made. The people I've loved.* No matter how fleeting this was, I need them to believe: everything mattered. This life was enough.

But it's not true, of course.

Nothing will add up to enough. I wish someone had told me that the end of a life is a complex equation. Years dwindle into months, months into days, and you must begin to count them. All my dreams and ambitions, friendships and petty fights, vacations and bedtimes with a boy in dinosaur pajamas must be squeezed into hours, minutes, seconds.

How should I spend them?

NO CURE FOR

BEING HUMAN

———

CHAPTER ONE

Best Life Now

I WAS IN BED IN THE SURGICAL WING OF DUKE University Hospital when the doctor popped his head in the door and smiled apologetically before flicking on the fluorescent lights. It was 4:00 A.M., the end of my second night in the hospital, but no one in a hospital sleeps in the conventional sense. There are only intervals of sleep without rest, interrupted by unfamiliar voices.

What's your date of birth? On a scale from one to ten, how would you rate your pain?

To this day, if you wake me up from a nap, I will immediately tell you my birthday.

I opened my eyes and saw a boyish face. The doctor

wore a white coat too large for his frame and his eyes were bleary either from a day that had only begun or from a night that had gone on too long.

"Six, sixteen, 1980. June 16."

"Right," the doctor said, then paused. "So . . . you're thirty-five."

I nodded, and my eyes began to water. I brushed the tears away quickly. *Not the right moment for that now, thank you.*

"If you keep replenishing my fluids, I'll just keep crying," I explained. "Maybe keep me in a stage of light dehydration for the next few days."

The doctor suppressed a laugh and began to riffle through my case history. "The patient has a history of abdominal pain after meals. Significant weight loss. Nausea and vomiting. No ultrasound evidence of gallstones or cholecystitis, but results of hepatobiliary scan led to a surgical consult to remove the patient's gallbladder . . . then you got a CT scan."

"No," I corrected. "I yelled at a surgeon for the first time in my life and said that I was not leaving his office without a scan. *Then* they ordered a scan."

This had been the biggest showdown of my life, the doleful surgeon with his arms folded and me loudly demanding some kind of treatment. It had been five months, and I had lost thirty pounds. I was doubled over with the pain. "I can't bear this much longer," I had said, again and again as doctors benignly shuffled me along.

The young doctor glanced up at me and then turned back to his notes.

"The scan revealed that the liver has multiple focal lesions; the largest are seen within the caudate and right hepatic lobe in addition to several scattered sub-centimeter lesions, some are noted within the periphery of the liver, and some are subcapsular. The large left transverse colon mass was what created the functional obstruction for you, hence the pain." He looked up at me quickly. "And then there are local regional lymph nodes that are worrisome for early peritoneal carcinomatosis."

The heart monitor beeped softly.

I cleared my throat nervously. "Um, so, this is my first real conversation since the diagnosis. I mean, I know I had surgery, obviously."

Flustered, I tried to start again. "The day before yesterday, a doctor's assistant called me on the phone at work to tell me that I had Stage Four cancer. But I don't know what these terms mean except that it sounds like I am a spaghetti bowl of cancer. People keep saying 'lesions,'" I said. "I haven't had a chance to google it. What are lesions exactly?"

"Tumors. We're talking about tumors."

"Ohhhhh," I said, embarrassed by another flood of tears. "Right. And are there more than four stages of cancer?"

"No."

"Okay, so I have the . . . most. The most cancer," I finished lamely.

The doctor stood there for a minute, raking his hands through his hair, whatever plans he had for this conversation deteriorating. He lowered himself onto the chair beside the bed but remained bolt upright as if to remind us both that he could leave at any time. The room was warm and stale. A silence folded over us, giving me a moment to look at him more carefully now, his mussy hair and anxious expression, wrinkled coat and brand-new sneakers. *He is too young for this. God, we are both too young for this.*

"I'd like to ask you some questions, if you don't mind."

"By all means."

"I'd like to know what my odds are. Of living. I'd like to know if I will live. No one has mentioned that." I kept my voice invitational. *I will not shoot this mes-*

senger. This is a friendly exchange between interested peers.

He paused. "I only know how to answer that by telling you the median survival rate for people who share your diagnosis."

"Okay."

"Based on the information we have about people with Stage Four colon cancer, the survival rate is fourteen percent," he said and began to scan the room as if looking for a window to climb out of.

"A fourteen percent chance of survival," I repeated in a neutral voice. My head felt suddenly heavy as if I were pushing the words up a steep hill. *Fourteen percent. Fourteen percent.* We lapsed into another silence. The doctor shifted in his seat. He rose to leave, but I reached out, abruptly, to stop him.

"Hey!" I said too loudly. "I mean, hey."

Startled, he looked down. My hand was closed tightly around his arm like a collar.

"It's just . . ." I started again. "You'd better be holding my hand if you're going to say stuff like that."

He sat back down and carefully took my hand. I closed my eyes and thought of the last time I was here, in this hospital, holding someone's reluctant hand. It was a maternity nurse. And I could not be reasoned with. "Short inhale! Long exhale!" she had shouted. "Are you laughing or yelling?" A bit of both. But I was waiting for something absolutely wonderful to happen.

I opened my eyes.

"Okay." I said, letting him go. He stood to leave. "Wait! Wait. Before you go. What does survival mean in this context?"

He paused, his expression softening.

"Two years," he said.

I don't know what he saw, but he took my hand again.

"Okay," I said at last. "Okay then." Because I was counting.

TWO YEARS. 730 DAYS.

This new definition of living is glued together by a series of numbers. I would be thirty-seven years old. I would celebrate my fifteen-year wedding anniversary. Zach would turn three.

I rummage around the things that the nurses had left within reach—a styrofoam cup of apple juice, peanut butter crackers, an untouched bowl of Jell-O cubes—until yes, there. My phone. I pull up the calendar and the calculator for some quick math: two Christmases, two summers, and 104 Thursdays.

I sink back into the bed with a long exhale. *That is not enough time to do anything that matters. Only small terrible choices now.*

Just then, Toban tiptoes into my hospital room holding a coffee so protectively that I already know the kind of night he has endured. I stuff the phone under my blankets and smile. Seeing me awake, he smiles back, a little nervously. A newly forming habit.

"Did I miss anything?" he asks, coming around to the side of my bed to press his cool palm against my sticky forehead. He frowns.

"No," I reply quickly. "There's nothing definite, I mean."

He settles into the chair and leans back, closing his eyes. I study him for a long moment. My husband has only ever had three facial expressions on his stupidly handsome face: brooding, sleepy, and what I call "trampoline face" which is the self-satisfied look of a grown man about to do a flip on a trampoline and hoping everyone will stop what they're doing to applaud. But now I can see we're adding another. Careworn.

Until now, we have been floating through time.

Look, this was the summer we fell for each other as camp counselors. It was an epic teenage love story starring two teenagers who held hands on the truck ride to the country dump to watch the bears eat garbage. I am forever grateful to the indulgent crowd who let a twenty-two-year-old bride sing the song "At Last" about her long road to the altar. Then this was the year I graduated. This was the year I graduated again. We dipped in and out of moments with reckless joy.

But now I am unsure. I want to say, *my darling, I am a clock, and I am ticking loudly.* But is this too much? Would it be worse if he knew?

I look around the room with sudden impatience. "Let's see if I can get out of here."

Toban opens one eye. "Let's not push it."

I exhale loudly so he turns his face toward me. "You've had a major surgery," he begins. "This is the moment to rest. Your parents are at the house taking care of Zach, so there's no need for you to rush home. Just . . . take your time." But he has no idea what that means to me now.

"That's the last thing I want to do," I say, firmly pressing the button to call the nurse.

—

MY HOSPITAL ROOM IS a turnstile of colleagues and friends, almost all of whom are pastors—and one bishop just to jazz things up—so they bless the crap out of me. They kiss my wet cheeks and bust out all the instruments that the church packs into its spiritual toolkit: prayers for healing and for peace; hands laid heavily on my shoulders and head as they invite God's presence; anointing oils that smell like Christmas, which they apply to my forehead in a greasy cross. I am convinced that by the time I am ready to leave the hospital, I will have acne there in the shape of a cross. I close my eyes when they stand around the bed, singing hymns with their naked voices. For a minute there, I am whole.

But then I am not. When they go, and I am alone again, I feel like I could scream, *this is criminal. This is a travesty. This is the end of the world.* But it isn't. It is only the end of mine.

I have been firmly instructed by my medical team that I will not be released from the hospital until I can eat solids and walk without falling over. So I set my mind to this with a determination that my father deems overzealous. Soon I can hobble to the door—before my sudden dizziness prompts a lot of speedy rescue by the nurses. I graduate to painful laps to and from the elevator, then trips up and down the hall, and, before anyone has been consulted, I discover the downstairs Starbucks and hospital gift shop.

I see now that it was probably alarming for the teenager at the gift shop counter to see a patient in a blue cotton gown wheel her own IV into the store, mutter loudly at a carousel of books, and begin to pull titles off the shelf. Not one by one. But dozen by dozen.

"I'd like to see the manager," I say to no one in particular. The teenager produces the manager, an older woman in an embroidered sweater, and presents her to me with wide eyes that tacitly suggest minimum wage doesn't cover this scenario.

"Can I help you, ma'am?" the manager asks gingerly.

But I am coming in hot.

"*Yes!* Thank you. I need you to know that these books are not suitable to be sold in a hospital." I point to the pile of Christian bestsellers I've made on the floor, books that I had carefully studied and documented in a comprehensive history of the movement known as the prosperity gospel. I spent ten years interviewing their celebrity authors and pulling apart their promises for divine happiness and healing with gentleness. But that's not what I am after today.

The manager only stares.

"Okay, like this one for example." I nudge *Your Best Life Now* with my foot. Televangelist Joel Osteen is on the cover, grinning and leaning into the camera.

"It says here it was a *New York Times* bestseller," she says reasonably.

"He's writing about the 'prosperity gospel.' He's saying God will reward you with money and health if you have the right kind of faith. Joel Osteen is America's most famous prosperity preacher." My voice is too high, even I can hear that.

The teenager pokes his head out of the back office and immediately disappears again. I take a deep breath.

"Normally, okay. I can handle this. But you can't sell this in a hospital. You can't sell this to *me*." I gesture melodramatically to my gown, and she looks away, as if to give me a moment of privacy.

I gesture to another book and then another. "*This*

book tells me to claim my healing using Bible verses. *This* one tells me that if I can unleash my positive thoughts I can get rid of negativity in my life."

"So what do you recommend instead?" Her back is to me as she starts to reassemble the display I have dismantled.

I glance around the bookstore. There are books on how to let go of the past, how to live in the present, how to claim a brighter future. I suddenly feel like I need to sit down.

"Just let me point out the books that actively blame people for causing their own diseases." Which she lets me do. The next time I wheel past the bookstore window, copies of *YOUR BEST LIFE NOW* have been replaced by copies of Joel Osteen's new book, *You Can, You Will*.

THAT LITTLE PHRASE "BEST LIFE NOW" is what Americans began using at the dawn of the twenty-first century to describe the satisfaction of mastering your life. Joel Osteen coined it in 2004, and, almost overnight, everyone from Oprah to diet gurus and Hallmark movie starlets reached for it as the gold standard. How did you know when you were truly living? You were living your best life now. You could see the fullness of your accomplishments spilling out of your Instagram account.

Taking the kids to Disneyland!

Surfing in New Zealand. Again. Does it ever get old?!

Happy anniversary, honey. You're my best friend, my soulmate, and my everything.

And according to every reality show I have ever watched, it is the only correct response if you encounter an ex-boyfriend and they coo, "But how *are* you?" *I am living my best life now, Matthew.* No explanation required.

The great triumph of the "best life now" paradigm was that it neatly summarized the promises of an entire American wellness industry: everything is possible if you will only believe. You can find this confident message everywhere from megachurches to Burning Man. It's expressed in the advertising around Peloton bikes and deluxe yoga retreats. Good vibes are big business.

Every year billions of dollars are pumped into a wellness industry defined by the theory that we can be perfected. We can organize ourselves, heal ourselves, budget ourselves, love ourselves, and eat well enough to make ourselves whole. In the 1970s, a New Age strain of America's famous self-confidence took hold of the boomer counterculture. Its promises were bold and metaphysical, insisting that the mind could overcome the sins of the therapeutic age: low self-esteem, mediocrity, and a ho-hum existence. Such was the flood of self-help books on the *New York Times* bestsellers list that, by 1984, the newspaper began siphoning them into a separate category to give other genres a fighting chance. Soon every good habit and self-improvement philosophy had the potential to become a fully-orbed commercial enterprise. What began as metaphysics was now packaged as science, backed by psychological expertise, lab results, and clinical stamps of approval.

Modernity is a fever dream promising infinite choices and unlimited progress. We can learn how to be young forever, successful forever, agents of our own perfectibility. We can fall in love with Tony Robbins and Eckhart Tolle, Joyce Meyer and Rachel Hollis. Women can learn that their better selves can be measured in Weight Watchers points, squeeze into Kim Kardashian's waist trainers, or be enhanced by the right shade of Mary Kay lipstick. Men can save like Dave Ramsey, master the habits of highly effective people, or flip a tire or two at their local CrossFit. The American admiration for bootstrappers and optimists became a capitalist paradise. Everyone is now a televangelist of the gospel of good, better, best. Harness your mind to change your circumstances. The salvation of health and wealth and happiness is only a decision away. Will you finally let it save you?

But I cannot outwork or outpace or outpray my cancer. I can't dispel it with a can-do attitude.

Many people believe that faith offers the one and only formula for living. We need not fear the uncertainty of life because God has a *plan*. There are two versions of this belief prevalent in America, each drawn from a different well of scripture, tradition, and experience. In the first, more therapeutic, account, God has a plan to make us happy. Influenced by the prosperity gospel and our self-help age, this version preaches that divine forces are participating in a loving conspiracy to keep us on an upward, chosen trajectory. God is nudging us toward careers, partners, and dreams which further our immediate and ultimate good.

In the second, more deterministic, account, God has a plan for our betterment, but not necessarily our happiness. Before the foundations of the earth, God foreordained our lives and directed our steps, and everything that may seem accidental or incidental, good or bad, will someday be revealed to be part of God's best hopes for us. But in the meantime, we will have to trust that the plan is "good" regardless of how it appears. We suffer. We are heartbroken. We lose more than we can afford. I have met countless suffering people who find this belief in God's plan to be deeply comforting. In this moral universe, God allows our sorrows to instruct us before drawing us into a heaven with no tears.

While I believe that there may be rich meaning at every crossroad in our lives—each meeting and departure, car accident or chance encounter—I do not believe that God will provide for every need or prevent every sorrow. From my hospital room, I see no master plan to bring me to a higher level, guarantee my growth, or use my cancer to teach me. Good or bad, I will not get what I deserve. Nothing will exempt me from the pain of being human.

Today will be as ordinary as yesterday, days and weeks working out the consequences of the moments that came before. We like to imagine that we are starring in an extended morality play where lessons are learned and the hero never dies. But, in fact, we must make do with the fact that there will be weddings and funerals again this year, and everyone will still spend most of their evenings watching Netflix.

This is a kind of freedom. The only question is how we should live under the burden of it.

I did not realize how much I wanted a blueprint for how to live until the day I was released from Duke University Hospital. I had pushed the doctors to let me go home, and I was elated to be leaving right up until the nurse pushed my wheelchair through the doors. When I saw Toban and my dad, fear hit me with the first blast of fresh air. They hopped out of the car and looked at me appraisingly, trading notes with the nurse about how to stand me up and sit me down again without tearing the stitches in my abdomen.

"Dad," I said, too quietly. *"Dad!"*

Toban was tossing my bags into the trunk and my dad was adjusting the front seat to give me more leg room. He glanced over.

"How will I know if I'm doing this right?" I said in a low voice.

"Doing what right?" he said, his head buried under the seat.

I am suddenly embarrassed by the answer.

"Live. I'm not sure I know how to do that anymore."

They stop short and turn to look at me. My father scratches his head and glances around as if searching for inspiration. Toban's face is creased with worry, his eyes cast down. All of us are far beyond what we know.

CHAPTER TWO

—

Timekeeping

MY HOUSE IS A HIVE OF PEOPLE TRYING TO
save my life by doing errands. There are a number of
Mennonites in my extended family, so I hail from a
long line of overworkers, famous for pacifism, sim-
plicity, and the foreboding sense that God is very dis-
appointed by naps. My mother devotes herself to
laundry while my father-in-law pokes at the rotten
boards in the fence. My sister-in-law immediately
finds her role as my nurse, which is convenient because she is one, and a tight regimen of pills and soft
foods must be kept. Zach races and roars between
them, leaping off of furniture and wobbling around

for a moment as if destabilized by the weight of his delightfully oversized head.

I watch them all, buzzing.

Is there anything else we should be doing? they wonder.

I call a family meeting to discuss our time together. We sit in a grim circle around the living room with additional friends and family calling in to hear my report. I explain that I will start chemotherapy soon and have a medical device called a "port" inserted in my pectoral muscle to ease the burden of the drugs on my veins. Until my incisions heal, however, we must wait. I want to tell them that these next months together may be all we have but I end up saying, "Thank you so much for coming. I am very concerned that we don't have enough towels."

There is a quiet speed to our despair. I drift in and out of sleep only to discover that another room has been cleaned and stocked and a flurry of meals prepared and distributed with military purpose. There is everything to do, and nothing to be done.

"Is this what a siege is like?" I ask one afternoon, my head resting on my father's soft stomach. What started as my childhood bedtime ritual ("Dad, who was the meanest king of England?") became an entire world we could live in together. On car rides or walks with the phone pressed hot against my ear, we would spend hundreds of hours pulling apart arguments ("How does literacy transform a culture?" "Why are monuments important to societies?") and lamenting how few people find Canada habitable.

He is, like me, a historian—someone who loves truth by analogy—so he knows what I am carefully, indirectly trying to say. I keep getting cards in the mail encouraging me to "fight" and "kick cancer's butt." But cancer is the enemy who is willing to wait outside the walls, and there is an army inside that must take careful inventory. What looks like a fragile peace is actually an invisible war.

We have had this conversation so many times— long rambling discussions about famous blockades of cities like Carthage, Jerusalem, and Leningrad. A conquering army has a fortified city surrounded for what might be days, months, or years. The people trapped inside begin with full pantries only to watch their bodies whittled down to sinew, burning furniture for warmth and gnawing on bread mixed with sawdust. A siege is a race toward disaster.

He kisses the top of my head.

"You have excellent troops, my dear," he says, pulling the blanket around me and tucking the ends under my feet. He sighs. "You and your mother. Refusing to wear slippers."

I snuggle in closer, allowing him this deflection.

I am whittled down now, shrunk to my adolescent weight. I can see the way my mom presses her lips together as she helps me into my clothes in the morning; my favorite pants are hanging loosely over my hips and the gauze taped across my blanched stomach keeps tearing strips off my skin. Those circles under my eyes are now a deep purple. We cannot speak it, but the truth hangs over us—that those who cannot fight back must race against time.

TODAY I AM MEETING my new oncologist, Dr. Cartwright. I met him briefly at the hospital, but at the time I was lightly hallucinating and telling strangers stories like "That Time I Accidentally Murdered the Show Poodle of a Former State Senator from Nebraska When I Brought Chocolates as a Gift and Left My Suitcase Open and the Dog Ate Them and Died When I Went to Buy Lobsters." That, combined with the frequent nudity of hospitalization, leads me to shake his hand firmly now and attempt some version of "I normally wear blazers."

We are sitting in unnatural silence in the Duke Cancer Center under the fluorescent lights of the examination room. I have crowded my father, mother, sister-in-law, and husband in a row of chairs along the wall while I am perched on the examination table, my shirt lifted so he can examine the surgical incisions and check for signs of infection. I glance over at Toban, his face drawn into a new, fifth expression— that of an astronaut suddenly released into space, drifting. It will take me months to recognize how fear looks on every familiar face.

The oncologist, satisfied by what he has seen, clicks on the computer monitor and begins to read my report.

"At first, the chemotherapy drugs will be potent, and then we will likely see a reduction in the size of the two largest tumors," he says. He is scrolling through MRI images, which reveal my organs slice by slice like an Easter ham.

"Here. See? There are two large tumors, one here and one buried deep by the IVC. And then we have these spots right here, here, and here."

We squint at the images on the screen. I return to scrutinizing the medical summary that the nurse has given me, but the sentences are heavy with unfamiliar words. I can only piece together that bad news has measurements, millimeters of tumor growth mapped onto segments of my organs. Apparently I should be concerned about the rim-enhancing masses in the right hepatic lobe and its proximity to the IVC. And there is some evidence of metastatic adenocarcinoma in the lymph nodes. I want to start with questions like "Where is my liver?" but we have floated too far from any language I know.

"I studied Latin in high school," I tell him, attempting to be charming. "After orchestra practice. I would go visit an old priest, and we would read Latin and listen to his wife play the harpsichord."

The oncologist is probably my age. We work at the same institution and maybe even went to the same universities. But he has perfected a disappearing act that I will come to recognize in doctors. Under his white coat, he could be anyone.

"People always assume the harpsichord is a really classy instrument, but it can't change volume. So it sounds like an unbelievably boring piano. Just plonk,

plonk, plonk." I mimic the soft hammer on the strings, already annoyed at myself.

He looks back at me blandly and then picks up where he left off.

He explains that it is too early to tell what any of this will mean. Chemotherapy will beat back the cancer's multiplying cells, but it must destroy them all within a certain time limit. Ten months, give or take. However, there are two other possibilities. There is a 7 percent chance that I have a condition which will cause cancer to multiply unabated, making any treatment impossible. It is an automatic death sentence. Or I might be part of the 3 percent of patients whose tumors are magically more likely to respond to a new kind of cancer treatment called "immunotherapy." His eyes look very bright when he says this.

"So, I maybe live, die almost immediately, or have some kind of magic cancer that gets special treatments?" I summarize.

"Pretty much," he says.

"Okay," I say. The hospital has already drawn blood and will notify me in a few weeks.

Late at night my mother will find me on the living room floor, surrounded by hundreds of pages of medical reports, trying to decipher their meaning. Hospitals are the last great archives, I tell her. Every drop of my blood has a paper trail. She wants to touch me, but I have arranged the paperwork around me in concentric circles like the rings of a dying tree.

"It is too much," she says.

"I know."

I pick up a stack of papers with both hands and shake them. I had been so overwhelmed by the end of the doctor's appointment that I felt drunk, slurring medical details and repeating things I had already said.

"I can't even read my own charts. All I can figure out is that cancer grew from my colon and is scattered across my liver . . . and that I am useless."

"You can't outlearn this, my love," she says gently.

"No. But mom, I need to try."

I USED TO EXPERIENCE time as productivity. Consulting checklists and packing lunches and yelling *"Remember to pick up laundry detergent!"* to no one in particular. I had invested heavily in the science of efficiency. I had streamlined my processes, refined my habits and adopted "proven principles." I poured more and more into less and less. Now I watch my friends and family head out the door for work, errands, anything, hungry for that feeling of being propelled through the world.

I am slowly realizing that I have been a human bulldozer since I was a child. My parents once returned from a trip to discover that I had renovated and staged their entire basement ("Did you know that wood paneling can be painted? I organized your record collection. I hope you weren't attached to the treadmill. It didn't work with the new floorplan.") Back from college for a weekend, I came extremely close to signing the paperwork for a cabin they did not yet realize they needed. Had they ever really considered the benefits of a four-door Toyota sedan? I oscillated between considerate and wildly presumptuous in my efforts to steamroll the shortest path between thought and action.

I always wondered if I felt so at home in America because of its famous love of efficiency, an ideal untarnished since the Industrial Revolution. I teach my seminary students about Frederick Taylor, a plant foreman at the Midvale Steel company in Nicetown, Philadelphia, in the 1880s. Marveling at how little he and his fellow workers managed to achieve in a day, Taylor developed an approach to the factory floor that, he believed, could improve the running of homes, farms, businesses, and churches. His ideas were soon adopted and adapted by the legendary Henry Ford, who revolutionized the automobile industry, and manufacturing generally, by breaking down complicated tasks into a series of simpler actions and units of time designed to increase productivity. Workers could now dramatically improve outputs by behaving like cogs in a single human machine.

When I explain this to my divinity students, I try to sound ominous. The virtues of mass production are seductive. Speed. Productivity. Growth. But the labor my students are preparing for is slow and inefficient. Most of the week will be spent trying to offer kindness to a deacon who never liked you, or weeding heresies out of the Sunday School material you bought online. You'll spend days coming up with enough beauty and truth to fill an hour on Sunday only to receive a dozen comments from parishioners about how much they miss the old pastor on their way out the door. If you want progress, take up running. If you want meaning, run a church. I say this with great solemnity before I rush off to a faculty meeting, where I will answer email with a lot of vigorous nodding to demonstrate my attentiveness. I deftly outmaneuver joys like naps in my attempt to winnow my inbox down to zero, garner perfect teaching evaluations, and immerse my toddler in Canadian folk music. I am a magician with a single trick: gather round and watch how this woman can take a solitary moment and divide it into a million uses!

But no one has seen me worship at the altar of productivity more than Toban. When I woke up one morning with a stuffy nose and sore throat, I accidentally took the wrong pills. Instead of the nondrowsy decongestant (a cheerful yellow pill), I had taken the nighttime edition. Toban found me sobbing over the toilet, desperately attempting to gag myself at 7:00 A.M.

"It was green! The pill was green, not blue!" I protested, half laughing and mostly crying.

"Why can't you just take a nap?" he asked sensibly.

"I have so much work I want to get done! *Why? Why* is this happening to me?"

Toban looked around the bathroom as if surveying a crime scene.

"Well," he said, "it looks like the real victim here is efficiency."

———

I HAD HEARD THE phrase "spending time" again and again without grasping its meaning. But since my diagnosis, I see that a well-spent day is a feat of accounting.

I set my alarm for 6:00 A.M. when the house is still, because some truths are only bearable alone. I lock myself in the bathroom, hold my breath, and try not to look as I unfurl the long strip of gauze folded up in my abdomen wall like origami, stained in a patchwork of bright crimson, milky yellow, and a wet blush. I carefully cut out a new dressing, stuff it back into the wide hole where my belly button once was, unpackage a syringe, and swiftly press the needle into my stomach near the incision. There are injection sites every few inches in an uneven row. I shake my head, pulling a baggy shirt over my stomach. *That's okay. You were never going to win any swimsuit competitions anyway.*

I start a pot of coffee to clear the mental fog of last night's medication, pile dirty clothes in the washing machine, and wait for Zach to stir. I love to be the one to find him puttering in his crib. In the calm of the almost dawn, everything is ahead of us. I will read him stacks of books about tractors and make sock puppets to demonstrate the love shared between two

pieces of farm equipment. He is the wonderful excep-
tion to my ruthless timekeeping. Minutes feel loose
and elastic. Breakfast is not simply the first, predictable meal after my alarm goes off. It is the long stretch
between changing diapers, trying to shovel mush into
an unwilling mouth, and then trying to understand
the speed and agility with which a toddler can remove
his sock and stuff it in his juice cup. Again.

The house is stirring as Operation Remove Apple-
sauce is already underway. Zach sits in a warm bath
demanding that his boats negotiate some kind of
treaty while I ease myself carefully onto the floor next
to the toilet to read a book about the history of wom-
en's ordination for my next academic project. Every
book during my maternity leave had needed to be
dried off and offered with considerable apologies to
the university librarian, but it was a suitable trade for
a few stolen moments of productivity and the chance
to sculpt Zach's hair into a soapy mohawk while he
laughed and made everything impossible.

But now I hold the library book in my hand for a
long moment, confused. *Am I still a writer?* My mind
is whirring, counting and recounting the months
ahead. I have a year and a half left to author a sub-
stantial volume that will secure me a permanent place

at Duke University, but I may die in . . . October, November, December, January, February, March, April, May . . . June. Nine months? I set the book aside.

By midmorning I have put Zach down for a nap and turned my mind back to this brokered day. I received good news from the hospital which has made everyone in the house a little sick with hope. I am among the 3 percent of patients with magical cancer. The remote possibility of a cure feels like helium, dizzying, surreal.

My oncologist was positively giddy when he handed me the information about the course of treatment for this magic cancer. Most cancer patients receive a cocktail of chemotherapies which fight cancer cells with blunt and terrible force. I am eligible to receive chemotherapy with an additional immunotherapy drug called Keytruda, but the medicine is still in the "trial phase" so I can only access it through a "clinical trial" in Atlanta, Georgia, a six-hour drive south. I feel unbearably lucky. This is the best medicine has to offer, and it is within my reach.

"Will my Duke insurance cover this?" I asked, trying to suppress my excitement before I became too hopeful.

He slapped his forehead. "I thought I had thought of everything!"

Was this a joke? Toban glanced over at me, mouth agape, but we quickly realized this was an Irony Free Zone.

Still, nothing can dampen our spirits. Any step feels like a step forward. And so Zach's midmorning naptime is now devoted to dead-end phone calls about insurance and thank-you notes to all the generous church friends and colleagues who are trying to help me afford weekly flights to Georgia if, by some miracle, I manage to be accepted into the trial.

I try to resume my role as the cheerful and tireless go-getter, but I fool no one. I am like a pocket watch that must be wound up again every few hours. I start confidently, but if I stand, someone in my family will immediately set a chair behind me. Every third hour I must take a small, round pill and, every fourth, some yellow pills wide enough to choke a pony. One makes my nose itch and the other makes me woozy, and none will make me eat. But this is the tick, tick, tick of cancer.

I have loudly decreed that rest is a "complete waste," so people attempt to trick me into leisure.

Oh, what a coincidence, a puzzle happens to be out on the coffee table. My father suddenly needs my opinion on a book he is finishing, would I mind skimming a chapter? My mother is at the stove, preparing sustenance for the winter months ahead like a doomsday bear, but there is absolutely no need for me to help her by stirring the pot. In fact, she'd rather I were sitting in the living room, where Toban attempts to swaddle me into a straitjacket of blankets.

In this new economy of scarcity I am skipping arguments, holding my tongue, sorting through the unfinished past for things that need to be said before it's too late. I am writing down internet passwords and canceling subscription services. In all my years learning the biorhythms of the "perfect day," conquering the morning routine, and charting my workflow, I had been racing toward the future along a single mental track. But now I must lay an entirely separate mental track headed straight for a cliff, and I find myself weighing each decision based on when I believe the road will end.

When Zach is finally in bed for the night, I live according to two rules. The first I borrowed from my father who, when he saw the 1971 classic film *The Trojan Women*—a not-so-cheery romp through the enslavement of a fallen ancient city—declared that he would never, never, never pay money to be sad again. So the No Unnecessary Sadness Decree takes effect after dinner every night, and television, movies, songs, and books are carefully screened for content.

I try to balance this with a second rule, the Gratitude Decree. I make lists of every good thing that has happened since the diagnosis: cousins, aunts, and uncles who came to visit, friends who sent cards, and tidbits about my health that feel like progress. I count my blessings with a blue dry-erase marker on a giant whiteboard and place it over the fireplace for all to see. I will try to remember these blessings at 2:00 A.M. when I am wide awake and my mind lurches toward the obvious: this is not enough. No matter how carefully I reframe painful experiences with a positive lens or focus my attention on tiny gains, I cannot make thankfulness the solution. And the harder I try to pin down my gratitude, the more it slips away.

I have been reading Zach his favorite story about a mother bunny who hops off in search of her baby bunny, wherever he has gone. The mother climbs mountains and sails the seas and teeters on a high-wire to pluck him from danger. And Zach loves to be greatly alarmed.

"Oh no!" he exclaims at the turn of each page.

"Don't you worry," I repeat, kissing the top of his delicious head. "Wherever you go, I will find you."

But now I am stumbling over these words. Every day we are speeding toward a future where I can't find him. I can see his feet straining against the velvety toes of his sleeper. He has started climbing over the side of his crib and chatting through his morning nap instead of sleeping like a brick. I am tenderly cataloging every detail as we learn to live with dwindling resources. The hours in each day will not amount to more rubber boots and winter coats. I will not be holding his soft tummy when he frantically pumps his legs learning to swim or staring at him in the mirror, nodding, as he concocts a plan to flatten his cowlick. For me, he will always be a toddler in a crib that his mother inherited from a friend.

"Are you borrowing this or is this for keeps?" the friend had asked as Toban loaded the frame into the bed of the truck.

"You'll never get this back," I said, laughing. "I've got plans."

—

CHAPTER THREE

Pragmatism

THE TRICK TO LOSING IS TO DO IT ALL AT ONCE.

It is our first visit and Peter the psychologist is listening carefully as I tell him about my sudden diagnosis. I cry most of the hour, and he hands me a tissue every five minutes until I have struggled through every word.

"I don't want to die." I plead with him like he decides these matters.

"No," he says gently. "Of course."

"And I am trying so hard to be honest with all of *you*." I flick my wrist in his direction.

"Me? Us?"

"You! Normal people! You know. People who assume they'll be fine."

He tries his best to look affronted, but we're both grinning.

"Sorry," I continue. "I'm not trying to be a jerk. But everyone seems to be proceeding under the assumption that their luck is guaranteed once they've hit . . . I don't know . . . middle class? No one seems to understand that everyone's life hangs by a thread."

Peter pauses thoughtfully. "You were saying earlier that your mind is always toggling back and forth between two tracks, one that is optimistic and one that is . . . realistic."

Realistic. My stomach twists.

"I hope for a future that might not come, and in the meantime, I have to make every decision count. It doesn't feel like there is much room for error here. What if I'm doing it wrong?" I shrug helplessly.

Peter says that he is not in the habit of giving advice, but he can tell that I won't settle for generalities. So he tells me that he learned a secret from hikers of the Appalachian Trail. People who dare to attempt the whole trail face down more than six months of lugging their belongings over more than two thousand miles of daunting terrain. Because eager beginners start their trek carrying heavy packs brimming with tarps and tents, cooking utensils and flasks and granola bars, that first stop on this long journey is the most important one. The hiker is already starting to flag, but they have only just begun. They have reached a moment of decision, the moment to ask, "What can I set down?" The extra cooking pot. The fleece hoodie.

"This will be a hard journey," he says. "Is there anything you can set down?"

The morning of my surgery to insert a chemotherapy port, I try to remember how much I will need to let go. I cannot stay as I am. Everything has changed and there is no turning back. I surrender my clothes to the nurses, pull a gown over my arms, knot it in the back, and climb reluctantly onto the gurney. I touch the slope of my sternum, feeling the smooth skin against my chest for the last time. And now a nurse is painting my skin in a yellow antiseptic and another is lightly puckering the veins in the crease of my elbow for a catheter.

I permit myself one thought: *this will only be terrible for a moment.* I can hear the careful preparations of doctors and nurses setting the surgical stage, feel them adjusting my heavy limbs and gown before gently placing an oxygen mask over my mouth. I imagine that I am at the end of a familiar dock, my toes curled over the edge, ready to dive into a glacier lake. Even in the heat of a Manitoba summer, water that cold demands complete capitulation as you are swallowed whole by a bottomless blue. Blue hospital gown. Blue surgical head covering. Blue starched hospital sheets up to my chin. Blue slipper socks that you somehow wake up wearing.

When the operation is over, when I can finally rise and am recovering at home, I move with purpose. Patting the unfamiliar topography of my bandaged chest, I shuffle to my closet and pull open the doors, yanking pieces of clothing out and throwing them into separate piles. Anything that cannot be stretched at the waist with an elastic band or a drawstring is gone; if it requires help from someone to fumble or yank or fuss, it is rejected; zippers and fine buttons and closures on the back, or necklines that will dip too low making fresh incisions visible, no. (For different reasons, I discard the black-and-white-striped shirt that, I am told, makes me look like a professional gondolier.) I keep anything that can be bleached of blood and saline, tumble dried on hot or taken off with one hand.

I hold up the last pair of elastic pants that I'd worn.

It had taken me four months to look robustly pregnant, pushing past the loathsome puffy stage and into a satisfying belly. I put them back on the stack of maternity clothes, soft to the touch, gently lift the pile out of the closet, and throw it down the stairs.

My father is grumbling on the first floor.

"Are you doing something useful? I've asked you to stop that."

My mother hops up the stairs and pops her head in the door. "What are you doing, sweetie?" She glances down at the debris with concern.

"Letting things go," I say evenly.

WHAT CAN'T YOU LIVE without?

North American culture has been obsessed with that question ever since they stopped having to worry about it. After World War II, an era of exuberant materialism emerged to serve the desires of the new, white, middle class. Parents saw their children raised in an economic summer, and their own Depression-era fears softened into anecdotes about hard lives, hard choices, and making do. My baby boomer parents spent their teenage years singing Beach Boys tunes in the middle of the prairies, thousands of miles from any ocean, and joyriding in borrowed Chevrolets the size of land yachts. It was the season to fill hope chests and line cabinets with wedding china.

We worship at the altar of plenty. Our heroes are corporate titans, fitness-empire builders, grinning televangelists, music legends, and decorated athletes whose gilded lifestyles and totalizing success hold out the promise of more. Twelve-car garages and infinity pools and walk-through closets and red-bottomed heels. Despite the boom and bust of the American economy over the last fifty years, we cling to stories of more-than-enoughness, believing the future is full to the brim for all of us.

Even the guides to living with the bare essentials are a kind of theater. Want to reduce clutter? Try the Marie Kondo method! Consider "simple living" in a rustic farmhouse with stunning oak rafters. Make sure to focus on your family by investing in a fully regimented schedule of children's hobbies: tap dancing on Tuesday, soccer on Thursday, and violin on Sunday. It's easy to imagine letting go when we forget that choices are luxuries, allowing us to maintain our illusion of control. But until those choices are plucked from our hands—someone dies, someone leaves, something breaks—we are only playing at surrender.

We heave with the collective exhaustion of excess, and yet we examine our lives item by item and wonder: *Is this it? Is this what I can't live without?*

Since my operation, I have been reduced to a steely pragmatism. Pragmatism is not simply an effort to be practical. It's a sprawling set of philosophical arguments, but the basic idea goes: start from the end and work backward. It is a simple criterion that is as American as baseball and reality-show romances. Substitute the phrase "Is it good?" with "Does it work?" Do what must be done, without the benefit of your preferences. Pain is a narrow gate.

I BEGIN THE BRUISING regimen of treatments in a clinical trial in an Atlanta hospital. Every Wednesday I leave my bed in North Carolina at 3:45 A.M., hop on a plane, and return home at midnight attached to a new chemotherapy pack and carrying a thick stack of medical reports I am learning to decode. My iron levels are dipping too low, something about my kidneys seems too high, and tumors dot my scans, shrunken but still stubborn.

There are things I cannot do without—things I do not have.

Money for treatment. My parents and siblings are taking out loans against their homes now and setting retirement ideas aside to help cover what insurance denies.

More children. I will not be allowed to have another baby; this is one of the many conditions attached to my participation in the clinical trial. The immunotherapies are so novel that when the doctor sends me the paperwork to sign, he forgets to hide the recent edits to the Microsoft Word document that appear in red font in the margins. Dozens of exciting horrors (projectile vomiting, yes please!) have been newly added to the list of anticipated side effects. More daunting is the actual bag of chemotherapy fluids that I must wear around my waist so drugs can be efficiently pumped into my system for several days each week. When this pack and its dispensing machine are strapped to my body, their rhythmic clicking sounds like a bomb preparing to detonate, warning off family members. My toddler, all noodly limbs and puckering kisses, is constantly being taken out of my arms to keep him from pulling at the tubes. I am toxic.

I must learn to tolerate the dizziness that comes from this kind of mental lifting. I buy an at-home Last Will and Testament, print it out on the home computer, and ask for a witness during dessert one night. After a physician's assistant at the hospital casually informs me that "the sooner you get used to the idea of dying the better," I make plans for a photographer to come to the house to take family portraits to remember me by. I smile brightly, my arms wrapped around them like a blanket, my husband, a toddler with overgrown bangs, and my mom tucked into my side fiercely blinking back tears. Only my father stands apart with his chin jutted like he is daring someone to punch him.

A pure pragmatism tolerates no sentimentality. I must be honest about the small math of how much a life is worth. How old are you? How much money do you make? How long have you been married? How many kids do you have? What's your zip code? I can hear it in the way people share my news with strangers: *She's thirty-five. Stage Four. Out of nowhere. Yes, a son. And she married her high school sweetheart.* In times of tragedy, everyone is an accountant.

And so I try to do the same. I make an appointment at Duke Human Resources to meet a woman named Linda, who will walk me through my employment benefits. I had already explained over the phone (quite reasonably, I thought) that I might die this year and I wasn't sure exactly what would happen to the benefits intended for my family. Would my son still be entitled to the school's tuition program for college? What would happen to the money tucked away for a retirement that wouldn't come?

"Maybe you should come into the office," Linda had suggested gently. "I'd be happy to gather the answers in the meantime."

Bureaucracies are automated systems made up of people who must choose each and every day whether their job will require any of their humanity. The week before I spoke to Linda I had been denied a handicapped parking pass at the Duke transportation office. Chemotherapy was giving me a nasty allergic reaction to the cold, so the doctor wrote me a note explaining that I couldn't walk long distances to my office in the winter. But, observed the transportation office employee sagely, the doctor's note said I couldn't *walk* in the cold. It didn't say that I couldn't *stand* in the cold. "Take the bus," he said, pushing the paperwork back at me. I had also begun to receive bills for tens of thousands of dollars for medical treatment denied by insurance, leading me to spend a day or two each week on the phone arguing with a cyborg whose primary function was to ask you to wait for a manager.

So when Linda greeted me by name at the door, asking careful questions and leading me to her desk, I felt a surge of gratitude. I explained how I had been in the final stages of securing life insurance before I was suddenly diagnosed and denied coverage, and now I was feeling a bit desperate, leaving my family this way. Linda gave me the only assurances she could, which were few, but she had found an additional list of financial information I should consolidate: bank accounts and passwords, retirement accounts and benefits, and health insurance member identification. Then she wrote something on the front of a folder and slid it across her desk.

"Put everything in this and keep it in a place where your husband could find it if you're gone. I've written my number here on the front where he can't miss it. I can help walk him through," she said, meeting my eye. The best person to have in a foxhole knows the cost of what must be done.

I FEEL PROPELLED FASTER and faster toward an end not fully in view. There is no plan for how many treatments I will have to endure. All I know is that every sixty days I will climb into a machine for the disease to be measured. The days on the calendar are rushing by. In the meantime, we have stood Zach against the doorframe to his bedroom to mark in pencil that he is a good inch taller than he was before. And in the short days outside of the hospital, I have painted narrow roads on our deck furniture so that Zach can run his toy cars up and down their length. This is the only kind of eternity I understand: how we can eat Goldfish crackers and lie in the hammock until the light fades, before deciding that dinner should be cereal again.

I have tried to solve the problem of finitude. I have tried to pour infinity into these stubborn hours. But I keep ticking. I used to hang over my son's crib as he slept, waiting for the moment that his eyelashes would flutter. He would fix his gaze on me, slowly. Taking his time, as if discovering me all over again on a Tuesday morning. But I can see now that I was mistaken.

What I remembered as moments were actually minutes.

———

CHAPTER FOUR

Bucket Lists

IT HAS BEEN SIX MONTHS AND EVERY WEEK IS the same. I fly to Atlanta to spend most of the day in the hospital receiving an infusion of chemotherapy or immunotherapy, sometimes both, while the clinical trial doctors gather data. *How much pain are you in? Can you still feel your feet and hands? Are the drugs still causing lockjaw? Any new side effects?* The blood work shows how close my organs are hovering to toxicity.

"Blast me," I say brightly when a doctor asks if I am ready to proceed. I will be the John McClane of cancer patients. The consent form clearly stated that patients who do not keep to their strict regimen will no longer be eligible to receive immunotherapy, and I'll be damned if I get kicked out of my trial because of some side effects. My feet are heavy and clumsy without much feeling in them, and the tips of my fingers are completely numb. I wrinkle my nose and find the sensation is gone there too, but I dismiss the thought. If this treatment fails, there is nothing else to choose.

Every sixty days I get my report card on whether I will be eligible to remain in the study. I lie in a whirring CT machine, dye coursing through my veins, and the doctors measure the blobs on the screen to see whether the tumors in my liver are growing. If they are not, the doctors smile. Praise God. I can stay in the study for another two months, take a deep breath and hope to start over again. I will probably do this for the rest of my life. Whatever that means.

My world I loved before cancer had its own measurements.

I am taller than my mother and shorter than my father. Where I grew up, we all murmured to each other, commenting on the amount of winter snow piling up against the houses and touching the eaves. We folded our arms and shook our heads, thinking about how the spring would bring floods and the summer would bring mosquitoes. These truths are so immutable that whenever my flight lands in Winnipeg, Manitoba, every friend and family member fights a primal urge to drive me straight to the floodway to show me the water levels.

"See?" they would cry. "Do you know what this means for the *mosquito count?*"

We relish the variety of new natural disasters, new calculations. Last fall, the wind and snow felled numerous trees, and, for months, no one talked about anything but branches. *Did you hear about the marathon? I heard it was canceled because of the sheer volume of sticks.*

As my father and I are waiting for my nurse to call me back for blood work, I tell him how much I miss familiar numbers.

"All measurements used to be done that way," he says without explanation. It is an old trick. He dangles a datum over an intellectual wormhole. I reach for it anyway.

"Like what?"

"Well, let's see." He settles into the plastic chair. "Take, for example, the human foot. We know what it looks like and generally how long it is, so people for centuries measured things according to how many shoe lengths a distance was. An inch was three kernels of barley. A yard was the distance between the English king's nose and the end of his thumb."

"What king?" I wonder, ignoring the sounds of nearby coughing.

"Henry the First. And then there was an acre, the area that a man and an ox could plough in a single day."

"What was a mile?"

"A thousand paces of a Roman soldier," he says without hesitation.

"Is that dumb? I mean, shouldn't everything be universal?"

"I guess it depends on whether everything that matters can even be counted."

My pager buzzes and the nurse is calling my name. The next few hours will be quantified in units of blood and saline and the cold prickle of chemotherapy pushed into my veins.

"It certainly feels like it, Dad," I say, disappearing behind the curtain of the nurse's station.

—

My precarious diagnosis has triggered a series of mental health assessments at the cancer clinic during which lovely and well-meaning counselors, all seemingly named Caitlin, are telling me to "find my meaning." They wonder if I should consider making a "Bucket List," as many other patients have found the process to be clarifying. What new skill could I learn? What classic movies should I watch? Is there a passion I might reignite? Cross-stitching? Restoring a vintage car? Soaring in a hot-air balloon?

I attempt to take notes while they are talking, but I find myself in a flurry of queries to the internet about the origin of the term *bucket list*, followed by a long period of processing my disappointment that it only became popular in the eponymous 2007 movie starring Jack Nicholson and Morgan Freeman. Boring. But I resolve to try to follow the lead of The Caitlins nonetheless. After all, what do I know about dying? I've never done it before.

On those merciful days without medical treatment, I begin to spend long afternoons in the stacks of the library digging through the history of the bucket list. The phrase itself is easy enough to date. In the eighteenth century, the term became a horrible reference to the act of either "kicking the bucket" from under your own feet (suicide) or having it knocked out from underneath you (homicide). But the idea that we should seek out a series of defining experiences is as old as our historical record. The ancient Greeks compiled a list of marvels known as the Seven Wonders of the World including the Hanging Gardens of Babylon and the Great Pyramid at Giza. Travelers in the Roman Empire could consult guidebooks to steer them to the home of the Greek philosopher Pythagoras and his famous theorem. With the ascendency of Christianity under Emperor Constantine in the fourth century came a different form of bucket list: the pilgrimage to places made sacred by Jesus and the saints. Churches and shrines were built over those places, and so began a holy travel circuit that believers have been making ever since. Throughout the medieval era, these roads were teeming with pilgrims setting out on epic journeys to see the many sacred bones, statues, burial spots, relics, and chapels scattered across Christendom, from Canterbury to Jerusalem.

A bucket list disguises a dark question as a challenge: what do you want to do before you die? We all want, in the words of Henry David Thoreau, to "live deep and suck out all the marrow of life." But do we attain that by listing everything we've ever wanted to do? Should we really focus on how many moments we can collect?

The idea of the bucket list captures the stirrings of our curiosity and wanderlust, devotion and enterprise, all of which pull us toward unknown adventure, but in its modern form the bucket list has become something else entirely. Here in the bowels of the library, I run the tips of my fingers along the spines of the hundred or so books with titles like *1,000 Things to See Before You Die*. It's a wonder that there are enough activities in the modern bucket-list industry to keep people industriously morbid. We have made bucket lists into a new form of experiential capitalism. Hang gliding. Snorkeling. Times Square on New Year's Eve and Paris in the spring. A successful life is one that can be completed.

The problem with aspirational lists, of course, is that they often skip the point entirely. Instead of helping us grapple with our finitude, they have approximated infinity. With unlimited time and resources, we could do anything, be anyone. We could become more adventurous by jumping out of airplanes, more traveled by visiting every continent, or more cultured by reading the most famous books of all time. With the right list, we would never starve with the hunger of want.

But it is much easier to count items than to know what counts.

All my life I have teased my mother mercilessly about the time she interrupted a raucous gathering of her daughters with this announcement: "Wait! One moment! Girls! I just need to tell you. Girls. Thank you for your attention. This will only take a minute. Girls, I wanted you to know . . . we have three kinds of apples." The produce drawer at the bottom of the fridge is open and my mother is gesturing importantly, but no one can hear her anymore because we are apoplectic. The phrase "three kinds of apples" lived in Bowler infamy, until, of course, I realized that in motherhood, the vast majority of my mental capacity would be consumed by inventorying items in case of emergency.

I am taking stock all the time. *Are we out of paper towels? Who is getting your mom from the airport? Did you remember your brother's birthday? I have to send this email by five p.m.* Each day sits in piles, there to be sorted between the things worth remembering and three kinds of apples.

"Make a list," suggests every Caitlin. "What are some things you want to do?" But I am excellent at lists. Lists of places to go. Dreams to interpret. Careers I might have enjoyed. Enormous statues I want to see. Languages I have learned and promptly forgotten.

Back in college, when I applied for a waitressing job at Perkins Family Restaurant, the manager read my résumé loud enough for the dishwashers to hear from the kitchen.

"You added something here under Additional Skills." He paused for dramatic effect. "You write that you are, quote, proficient at ancient Greek and Latin with a good reading knowledge of German and Russian. But you regret that your French is, again I quote, not what it used to be." He put the résumé down and rubbed his face with his hands.

And so began my midnight shifts to welcome drunk college guys stumbling home from a nearby bar called Coyotes.

"*Bonjour! Willkommen!*" I would greet them.

What a gift to waste a summer talking to sloppy boys and building towers out of the dessert menus behind the hostess stand—to have the time to join a terrible garage band and put a snowmobile through the ice more than once. What a privilege to have stories to burn.

We are grass, murmur the scriptures. Our crowns are just flowers. We are here and then gone in a burst of wind.

But I want things. I want more stories. I want life itself. But am I unfaithful in clinging so tightly to life? The disciples who ate with Jesus spread the news of his life in empires far from home, deeds of faithfulness for which they were promptly crucified, stoned, clubbed, or burned alive. Christians tell stories about how faith is like the smallest mustard seed that, once planted, grows into the mightiest tree, offering shade to the birds of the air. But here I wither in the heat of a cloudless day.

But should I want anything at all when my God says, let it go. Let it all slip out of your hands.

A few years ago, my student's dad discovered that he was in the last months of life. Much to everyone's astonishment, his father didn't have a wish list. In fact, his father didn't wish for anything at all. Not a trip. Not a meal. He sat contentedly in his overstuffed recliner in the living room humming about how much he loved his family. I think back on this story and wonder: Do people age into acceptance? Is this personality or maturity or a natural realism? Had he already accomplished what he wanted to do? Did he see his kids get married, reach an anniversary, or hit a milestone? What amounted to enough?

"I don't feel that way," I tell all the Caitlins, matter-of-factly.

I once asked my father what he would choose if he could see only one thing on his bucket list, and he said, easy: Troy. The ancient city was thought to be a fantasy conjured up by the mind of Homer until the 1870s when an amateur archeologist and profiteer named Heinrich Schliemann dug it up himself. And this story was enough to spur my father, a young boy in and out of foster care, to want a historian's life of grand discovery. And he did eventually get to Troy.

"Here I am, looking at it, quoting poet Alfred Tennyson about the ringing plains of windy Troy," says my father, tapping on a photo on his phone as we are waiting for one of my appointments. He was wearing an explorer's hat for the occasion and pointing off camera, clearly mid-sentence.

"You accomplished your dream, Dad."

"Right. Then everything was over."

"Your life spiraled into an immediate and precipitous decline?" I chuckled.

"Of course," he said, putting his arm around me. "I had children."

I AM LEARNING THIS universalizing language of medicine, its precision, its neutrality.

For months I have been vigilant about my doctors, alert for any nuances in facial expression or vocal inflection. *Is it bad? Is it worse?* The handful of times when I cried, or asked a particularly unvarnished question, I watched my clinical trial doctor retract like a salted slug.

The question "Yes, but will I live through the summer?" was answered by a flat monologue about the number of chemotherapy treatments I had received—and will yet receive—followed by a careful description of my blood work and then a rereading of my last surgical report. When the doctor concluded his speech, he clicked off the monitor of the computer as if to signal that there was nothing left to say. I desperately wanted to know how to turn a unit of time into meaning. And he would only tell me what was quantifiable.

But I am catching on, slowly working my way through research papers, taking note of unfamiliar terms, in the hopes of returning with the kind of questions that will give me the answers I need. I nod at my doctors thoughtfully and sit with them casually, the suggestion of collegiality between us now. These visits and scans are an opportunity to discuss what "we" are learning about "cancer."

In airports and in waiting rooms, I'm reading a book about the French Revolution. I am learning that when it comes to the modern obsession with quantification, I can blame the French. It was the Age of Enlightenment, and time itself was considered an arena of progress, a moral procession toward perfectibility. But devising a society based on uniform abstractions had a steep cost. Take, for instance, the map of France itself. The country had long been composed of twenty-six provinces of various dimensions, separated by mountain ranges and fused together by ancient tongues and trading routes and shaped by rivers wearing channels to the sea. Then their new state geographers laid the map of the country on a Cartesian grid and—*voilà!*—the provinces were abolished and replaced by eighty-nine *départements* of approximately equal size. If looked at from the sky, the new borders were neat. Elegant even. But from below, the world had been remade without reference to common history, language, or custom. It's true that when you deal in abstractions, you save yourself the trouble of having to learn the particulars, but, as in the geography of France, what is meaningful gets replaced by what is merely rational.

The universal, as it turns out, is rarely universal. When the French revolutionaries tried to rename the months according to the weather, they were actually only describing the climate in Paris. When they decided what constituted the measurement of a meter, they were calculating one ten-millionth of the distance between the equator and the North Pole as drawn through their own capital. The calendar year was split into twelve months of thirty days each, which would have been fine if that were the actual length of the earth's journey around the sun. A new metric system ushered in a system divisible perfectly by ten. There was even a short-lived attempt to decimalize the clock with one hundred minutes to the hour, but the church bells—the ones that they didn't melt down into cannons—continued to keep village life moving every sixty minutes.

I can feel the cost of all this abstraction late on Wednesday evenings, before my flight back home has boarded, when I tuck myself under an airport escalator to cry. I rendered myself intelligible—reasonable and quantifiable—to the round-robin of medical professionals so that I could understand the significance of what was happening to me. But now I can hear myself choking on the remainder, on the part that cannot be neatly quantified. I am somewhere in this vast expanse of data—blood count, tumor millimeters, survival rates—but none of it tells the story. Born here and grew up there, tried this and became that. Someone's kid, someone's friend, the mom of someone who will not recover from her absence. But I am a number here, open to infinite interpretation.

AFTER MONTHS OF TREATMENT and scans, treatment and scans in an endless loop, we are dizzy. Should we celebrate my thirty-sixth birthday like it's my last? Would we do anything differently if we knew? Now that my mortality is no longer an abstraction, my parents, my friends, Toban, are all looking at me to decide what these moments mean.

Do they look to me because I always used to have a checklist in hand? I would achieve tenure, master the

Russian language, and visit the world's largest statue of Paul Bunyan and his majestic blue ox, Babe, in Bemidji, Minnesota.

I resolve to try again, if only to create a little direction. Maybe we could visit the World's Largest Outdoor Ten Commandments in North Carolina—one of which has a spelling mistake. I fish around for inspiration in old journals and find a list dating back decades. Getting ready for bed one night, I pull out the old list and lay it flat on the comforter. It stretches across many pages in blue ink, pencil, then a red scrawl as new fantasies were caught and bottled like fireflies.

#5   See the pyramids.
#16   Take a scooter tour around Prince
      Edward Island.
#42   Publish a book.
#81   Make decent bread.
#86   Explore Venice with my parents.

"Does this count as a Bucket List?" I ask Toban. Tucked in bed, I am carefully arranged on pillows to keep my weight off the chemotherapy infusion pack. I turn to face him fully, which involves more shifting and harrumphing and rearranging of blankets.

I had been keeping lists like this since the eleventh grade, when I was spirited away with other earnest teenagers to a conference center for a leadership program. We built bridges out of masking tape and copies of the *Winnipeg Free Press*. I found plausible reasons to hide in the bathroom instead of holding hands with beautiful, beautiful Scott Stewart in an icebreaker game as it was well-reported that I had sweaty hands. But the culmination of the weekend was the rousing speech by a former Canadian football player who was making the rounds as a "life coach." We would need to become winners, he said, like a ragtag group of young men he once knew who, in 1990, won the Canadian Football League's highest honors as the Grey Cup winning team. Go Blue Bombers! Wait, did he mention that he *was* one of those men? We cheered. We learned about running our own plays in the Game of Life. Then we were instructed to write down specific goals to achieve before our clocks ran out.

"Ah, there it is." I point to the page, holding it up for Toban to see. "Number three. Perform a cello solo. In high school, that was the biggest dream I could imagine. I wanted to win an orchestra competition where the prize was to play with the Winnipeg Symphony Orchestra." Eventually I had lost badly and was forced to watch from the audience as the winner, in an impossibly fluffy ball gown, sawed through Tchaikovsky in a flurry of bow strokes and crinoline.

"But number five. See the pyramids." I sigh. I had been preparing to see the pyramids since elementary school, when my sister Amy and I learned Egyptian hieroglyphs and sent each other secret notes that read *jackal, scarab, bread, bread, bread* because we had misunderstood that the images should be read phonetically and had largely used them to ask my mom for snacks. For years afterward I wrote school essays about my future career in Egyptology, until I discovered that the great pyramids had already been plundered.

I return to paging through the list; I pull out a pen and check off a few as I go. We did, in fact, buy a hot tub. I had planted that herb garden. And the previous spring we had fulfilled my parents' dream of traveling together to Venice, learning to accept the merits of squid ink pasta, and emotionally investing in the rise and fall of a coastal empire. I strolled beside canals picturing return visits while they cheerily said their hellos and goodbyes to each monument and cobbled square.

"When I wrote this list I wasn't trying to imagine wrapping up my life. I suppose I was just . . . dreaming." I trail off.

"Oh, honey." He wraps his arms around me, careful with the wires and tubes. There is so much more silence between us now as we walk closer to the edge, but I can hear my heart thrumming in my ears as I imagine crawling out of my own throat, out of this body, away, away, away.

It had not occurred to me, until now, that life's wide road narrows to a dot on the horizon. I enjoyed the multiple somedays I learned to conjure up as a spectacularly unpopular child with a useful imagination. For several summers, I dreamed up a life on a farm on Prince Edward Island so I could attend a country school with Anne of Green Gables and her kindred spirits. I slept with clothespins pinching the tops of my ears for only a week before my mother convinced me that I would never achieve the elfin features of another L. M. Montgomery heroine. "Bowler ears are a life sentence, I'm afraid," said my mother, so I grew out my hair. I practiced sailing knots, memorized the parts of a ship, and chapped my hands learning basic knife skills in preparation for seafaring as a mistreated English orphan who craved a life of freedom. I founded the "Best Friends Writing Club" to allow other twelve-year-olds to decline the opportunity to read my original works about a fierce young huntress with an unshakable bond with Artemis, her horse. On the surface, I was living in a squat bungalow on the prairies through a seven-month winter. I was subject to my father's insistence that ground beef and a can of vegetable soup was a viable dish called "hamburger soup goop." But I lived many lives nonetheless.

I did not understand that one future comes at the exclusion of all others.

I had wanted two kids.

I had wanted to travel the world.

I had wanted to be the one to hold my mother's hand at the end.

Everybody pretends that you only die once. But that's not true. You can die to a thousand possible futures in the course of a single, stupid life.

———

CHAPTER FIVE

YOLO (You Only Live Once)

CHELSEA AND I ARE SITTING AT OPPOSITE ends of the table, and we can barely hear each other over the deafening music, but I am excellent at lip reading and understand that she wants me to eat one of her Peruvian tacos.

The music fades for a minute, and she shouts *"Take this stupid taco!"*

I yell back, *"Fine! Send me the taco!"* and so the taco begins to be passed, person to person, down the table. *"This is not a terrible idea!"* I shout. *"I do not have a compromised immune system and am very happy to have you all, individually, touching this food!"*

A friend with a doctorate in public health chimes in.

"From a public safety standpoint, I cannot condone what is happening right now!"

"You only live once, right?" I say holding the taco's wet remains in my hand, attempting to hoist it in the air like a beer mug. *"Here's to Chelsea! And another year. And more piñatas."* She has been my best friend from around the time that we began crying in the bathroom at school dances. And tonight I throw her a birthday party that devolves into incoherent yelling and the loud insinuation that I will die this very night, felled by the health complications from this compromised taco.

It is a perfect evening, until a casual acquaintance turns his chair toward me.

"So, you have colon cancer," he begins. This is how it always starts, with emotional tourism.

"Yup, me and every eighty-year-old man," I reply lightly, looking around the table for a natural segue. It's been one year since the diagnosis but this is still always the first stop on the small talk train.

"You should go out with a bang!" he shouts. The music has picked up again. *"I mean, since you're going to die. You should really live it up and go out with a bang."*

I think he, like the ancient poet Horace, is trying to say that we should all seize the day, carpe diem! Live now! Buy a boat! Bathe in champagne! Yell at a woman at a party?

I open my mouth to say something clever or frank but nothing comes out, just a little shake of my head. I stare at him, then make a beeline for the bathroom.

To so many people, I am no longer just myself. I am a reminder of a thought that is difficult for the rational brain to accept: our bodies might fail at any moment.

A friend came back from Australia with a year's worth of adventures to tell and ended with a breathless "You have to go there sometime!" Then he lapsed into silence, seeming to remember suddenly that, at that very moment, I was in the hospital. And I didn't know how to say the future was like a language I didn't speak anymore.

"The world is not safe," I will tell Chelsea later that night, crying on the floor of the restaurant's bathroom. "The world is not safe for people in pain."

"No, muffin," she says gently. "It's not."

"But there was a second there, Chels," I say, using my sleeve to wipe what is left of my eyeliner off my cheeks, "when I felt like myself again."

For just a few moments before I finished yelling about the lethal taco, I had not felt like a casualty of either the past or the future. I had been allowed to soak up the present like everyone else. Eat, drink, and be merry—because, you know, noroviruses.

THE MAXIM "LIVE IN THE MOMENT" is ancient wisdom repackaged. Don't worry, be happy. Hakuna matata. You only live once. It is the marrow of hedonism—that centuries-old philosophy rooted in the pursuit of pleasure—and the hope of every college student. Gather ye keg stands while ye may. Heaven seems distant when paradise is now.

There are versions of this philosophy which are, of course, pure idiocy. For the sake of my poor mother, I like to refer to my moronic choices obliquely, with words like *hitchhiking, abandoned mine exploration,* and *Nicaraguan rum.* Living in the moment can make us careless and materialistic, selfish and prone to wanton acts of never taking a multivitamin. Why recycle? Why save for retirement? Tomorrow is nothing but happiness deferred.

But in this digital age of exhaustion and distraction, the ability to be present-minded has become a rare and valuable commodity. My inbox is flooded with newsletters explaining how various philosophical, religious, and psychological strategies of mental self-management will help me embrace the fullness of each day, unfolding each moment like a gift. Our therapeutic culture swears this is freedom: freedom from our dizzying thoughts and our conflicting emotions as we exorcise the demons of negativity and desire. The latest bestseller might have gleaned an insight from Buddhism or the ancient philosophy of Stoicism, stripped out the underlying doctrine, cosmology, and ritual, and made the secrets of cultivated detachment, radical acceptance, and a calm mind available at rock-bottom prices. In this new strain of heroic individualism, people master the world by conquering their own inner worlds.

I try to sew myself into the moment with its needles and white blood cell counts, diaper changes, and grocery pickups. I read treatises on healthy expectations, mental disciplines, and acceptance of what I cannot change. But even as I resolve to keep myself in the present, the future keeps interrupting. I am scrambling to find Zach a larger onesie or discovering that next Christmas will probably become the season of "Please don't pull that off the tree." I have promises to keep to my best friend in the spring: a drive to the coast of North Carolina to show her the World's Largest Frying Pan.

I want to believe in the beauty of eternity, the endless future spooled out before us all. Time is a circle, the Christian story goes. It focuses on an image of God as the ultimate reality beyond time and space, the creator of a past, present, and future where all exists simultaneously in the Divine Mind. We are wrapped into a story without clocks. It is quite a mind-bender. Jesus arrives as a newborn with parents and a bedtime and so the Christian understanding of what is forever and what is chronological bends around him. God is eternal, but Jesus never made it to middle age. Jesus was born around the year 4 B.C., but was also hanging around when God created the heavens and the earth. Part of the mystery of the Trinity—Father, Son, and Holy Spirit—is that we believe the divine is behind us, with us, and before us. We are pulled toward eternity believing that God is already there.

But all of that feels useless. All I have is now.

I try to explain this to my friend Warren, an esteemed reverend-doctor who wears his clerical collar even on Mondays. After a long departmental meeting that I attend out of sheer boredom, I tell him that I have given up on the future.

After a long pause he asks, "Would you agree that true happiness is the ability to enjoy the present without anxious dependence on the future?"

"I'm really hoping you are going to tell me that Jesus said that," I say. "This is a trap, isn't it?"

"That was Lucius Seneca, the ancient philosopher of Stoicism," he says, laughing. "Look, it takes great courage to live as if each day counts. That was a fundamental insight of Stoicism. But we Christians are a people who must live into the future."

I have no idea what he means. The future is a cliff.

THIS IS MY ETERNAL present. It's Wednesday. I fly to another city as dawn breaks. I live at the hospital all day, which always smells like burnt grilled cheese sandwiches. They saddle me with a take-home pack of chemotherapy fluids. I fly home after midnight. The chemotherapy fluids are pumped into a plastic insert in my chest for the next three days. Rest for seventy-two hours. Then, too soon, it's Wednesday. Do it all again.

I emerge from every cycle of my medical treatment

grateful, weary, and, almost imperceptibly, weaker than the week before. After nine months of this, my face is bloated, sallow. A toenail comes off in my sock, and I hide it from Toban out of sheer politeness. The clinical trial doctors have stopped giving me one of the chemotherapy drugs because it is causing so much numbness that I can no longer tie my shoes or braid my thinning hair, but, mercifully, no one has said anything about kicking me out of the study. No one is saying much about my future at all.

I reach out to my first oncologist, Dr. Cartwright, at Duke's Cancer Center, with a vague hope that my immunotherapy drug will someday be available there, so I could stop traveling to Atlanta to take it.

"Yes, let's talk about getting you back to Duke," he replies smoothly.

A month later Dr. Cartwright sends me a note of congratulations. He has been able to make an arrangement with Merck, the pharmaceutical giant, for access to the immunotherapy drug here at Duke, and the news fills me with a bright hope. No more 3:45 A.M. wakeups. No more hours on the phone with airline companies, trying to fix a haywire flight—or relying on donations to afford the flights in the first place. A painful chapter of my life will finally close.

But my first oncology appointment back at Duke is not the homecoming I expect.

Dr. Cartwright sits on the stool in the examination room with my chart, looking it over with intense curiosity.

"Oh!" he exclaims after a great deal of murmuring and paging through the sheets. "You were quite the little lab rat, weren't you?"

Toban and I stare at him dumbly.

"But I didn't have a choice," I stammer. "If I didn't take all the drugs they gave me, they were going to kick me out of the study."

"Clinical trials are quite strict, yes. We have the ability to do things differently from now on." He proceeds to explain that I will no longer need to be attached to a chemotherapy infusion pack because I can take the same drugs in pill form. I blink back tears. He will also significantly reduce the level of chemotherapy.

"That's so wonderful. Thank you so much," I breathe, hardly able to process this good fortune.

Dr. Cartwright is still talking in a low voice, something about how I'm not the only one anymore. He has been treating a young patient like me for months now.

"You have another young patient on immunotherapy? Here at Duke?" I repeat slowly, as Dr. Cartwright chats amiably about how he had managed to secure the same drug for him too. *Months ago*. Months that I have spent traveling to Atlanta, whittling down my family's savings and relying on the charity of others. Months of arguing with insurance companies—because the treatment was administered out of state—contesting payments and fielding phone calls with bill collectors over clerical errors. I have been hooked to a bag of chemotherapy fluid that could have been administered by pills? I have been getting on a plane when I could have been walking down the hallway in my own institution?

I exchange confused looks with Toban, and we turn back to the doctor.

"But I thought you were my doctor too," I say, uncertainly.

"I am your doctor," he says bewildered. We appraise each other for a moment as if not entirely sure we are part of the same conversation. "And I worked really hard to get you access to immunotherapy at Duke. But we had to keep you in the clinical trial for at least six months out of respect for the trial."

"No, I'm grateful," I reply, chastened. "I'm sorry. I am grateful. I think I didn't understand . . ."

Before I leave, he draws me a little graph. I am approaching a threshold, he explains. My chemotherapy drugs are losing efficacy and if this immunotherapy isn't able to fight the cancer alone, I will begin a different chapter in my treatment.

He doesn't say the words, but I stare at the scribbles on the paper in my hands. His blue pen has traced a long line showing the predicted growth of the cancer if the immunotherapy doesn't work. The line soars up, up, up and away, taking everything with it.

How long can we put our futures on hold?

In high school I spent a luxurious amount of time crying in the hallway after math class about how terrible I was at algebra and how my grades would never qualify me for a scholarship to go to the Canadian university that Anne of Green Gables attended. (That she was a fictional character never deterred me.) Mr. Boothe, the math teacher, would pop his head out the door and yell something like "That B minus is not the death of your dreams, Bowler."

I did not believe him, but I loved him nonetheless. He wore a long white lab coat every single day of his working life so he could use the entire length of his arms to wipe off the chalkboard, sighing heavily at our unwillingness to stop being teenagers.

"This graph rises and falls like a wave, crossing the horizontal axis like *this,*" he'd say, drawing a series of smooth curves. "But *this* graph is a torrent of undulating lines, crisscrossing, making it the *sexiest graph of them all*." He'd draw quick lines across the board, arms flailing, before he'd stop and spin around to fix us with a leveling stare.

"You're not ready," he'd conclude with obvious disappointment, using most of his arms and torso to erase the chalkboard. We weren't. Years later, I wrote him a postcard from college admitting that, despite all evidence, his work in the service of my education (and the scores of undeserved letters of recommendation he'd penned) had propelled me toward a greater future. Despite long bouts of mediocrity, I was attending a dreamboat college.

A few months later I received in my campus mailbox a cheerful reply that he had decided to teach math overseas on his own grand adventure and had used my postcard as his own letter of recommendation. He died soon after. He was fifty-six.

I used to think that "adulthood" was a stretch of eternity that began shortly after college. In college, you learned what profession you were going to be and that was the end of it. I would only learn later that adulthood contains many lives, that you can dream and reach for more but that you will be kept busy managing kids who roll their eyes when you use your body like a human Kleenex as if you don't know how funny that is. I imagined that adults were people who ate and breathed and worked in the world they had inherited from centuries before. It never occurred to me that every life must be constantly reinvented by adventures and private jokes, and that it might, suddenly, end.

The ancient Stoics knew this. They knew that life is as fragile as a soap bubble. They lived in a world of invasions and sieges, cholera and smallpox. Husbands buried wives, and mothers buried children, and only prophets dared to speak about the future with a measure of certainty. In their world, it made sense to live each day as if it was their last. But the world I thought I knew before the diagnosis was hygienic, predictable, and safe—kids got vaccinations, people grew old, and everything else just required anesthetic, antiseptics, or whatever else my mom kept in the cardboard box under the bathroom sink.

Now the only moment that makes any sense happens in the predawn hours when I hear a small boy stirring. I pull him to my chest as if we were magnets kept apart by an unfeeling law of nature.

The terrible gift of a terrible illness is that it has, in fact, taught me to live in the moment. Nothing but this day matters: the warmth of this crib, the sound of his hysterical giggling. And when I look closely at my life, I realize that I'm not just learning to seize the day. In my finite life, the mundane has begun to sparkle. The things I love—the things I should love—become clearer, brighter.

Burdened by the past, preoccupied by the present, or worried about the future, I had failed to appreciate the inestimable gift of a single minute. I didn't realize that one second you can feel like chaff and the next you can be at a wedding reception and your friend Ally is gliding across the dance floor on a drink cart pushed by her husband, who is yelling "We are never going to die!" He started out saying it ironically, but, by the end of the night, we are starting to believe.

When I was first hospitalized with cancer, my friends sent me a photo taken of us that night. We're in party dresses, arms around one another, mussy hair, tears streaking mascara down our cheeks from a night gone a little wild. Maybe for a second there, I could have sworn that the universe slowed and stopped just long enough to watch me catch my breath.

Moments like these feel transcendent, the past and the future experienced together in moments where I can see a flicker of eternity. Time is not an arrow anymore, and heaven is not tomorrow. It's here, for a second, when I could drown in the beauty of what I have but also what may never be.

Hope for the future feels like a kind of arsenic that needs to be carefully administered, or it can poison the sacred work of living in the present: taking my medication, asking about a friend's terrible boyfriend, and inhaling the smell of my son's skin as he sleeps next to me. I want to be alive until I am not.

There will never be enough of these moments for me. Enough anniversaries with the man who still thinks that late adolescence was an acceptable time to get married. Enough pages of history books I scribble and then immediately send to my father, who will put on his glasses and squint at the screen impassively until he loudly declares it to be *"Quite acceptable!"* Enough early mornings feeding spoonfuls of glop into my son's mouth between our fits of giggling. And if those are the measures of time, I am bankrupt.

Once every few hours I pause what I am doing because I can't take a breath. I have caught a glimpse of the terrible someday when, even though I am his mom and he is my son and those words keep the birds in the sky, I may not be able to hold him.

I prepare for these moments each night, wide awake, imagining a time when I will be gone, even from his memory. When he will not know the weight of my hand on his blond head. He will wonder which of his features are mine (his mouth) and what traits started with me (his evil laugh). He will be at a party and someone will say, "You remind me of your mom" and he will feel a pang that a stranger knew me and he did not.

I canvass everyone I know who has lost a parent to find out what stories they cherish, and I incessantly google articles about long-term memory in children. Exactly how old does he have to be to find me in his memory? And what work do I need to do to be remembered? I put this question to my psychologist, who shakes his head.

"Kate, you are laying the foundation. It's there, but, yes, you might not get to see what he builds on top of it. The foundation is the part that doesn't show."

IN A MUDDY ATV on the bumpy ride up the mountain my friend Katherine and I chat with our yin and yang of Appalachian tour guides. One, a young man, is wonderfully unbathed and grins often, unselfconscious about the fact that he has lost or chipped most of his good teeth; the other, a fresh-faced blond woman, looks like she has stepped from the cover of a rock-climbing magazine with a hydration pack she'd be willing to share. Almost numb from my fear of heights, I silently vow to have the woman double-check my safety gear as the scraggly one gives me a pep talk about living life to the fullest.

"What does that look like for you . . . *whoa!*" I yelp. We bounce off our seats as he takes a hairpin turn and, unfazed, stomps on the gas pedal a few times as if checking to see if it has stopped working. I glance back at Katherine with wide eyes, and she shakes her head incredulously.

"Why do we have heavy gloves? Aren't there brakes for the zip line?" I ask.

"Your hand is the brake," he says cheerily, ducking a branch as we race by.

"What if my hand isn't a brake?" I say reasonably. "What if I can't stop as I'm hurtling toward the finish?"

"If you're not going to try then I'll have to take you down the mountain now," he says, furrowing his brow.

"No, I'm not saying that. I'm just saying, *what if.* What if I hit the end without stopping?" I ask. "I'm absolutely terrified of heights. What if I panic?"

"Oh, well then. It will feel like a car accident," he says pleasantly, stopping the car. "We're here!" And he hops out. By the time we have reached the top of the forested mountain, adjusted our harnesses, and peered over the edge of the first platform, he has carefully cataloged the twenty-five years of his life: the town where he grew up, his ping-ponging between adventure-seeking jobs, and his move to the mountain with his girlfriend in order to "live freely."

"Is it working?" I ask, letting him make the final tugs on my harness. "Do you feel free?"

"Lately I'm feeling a little bogged down. I came here with only one garbage bag of stuff. But now I have two." And with that he flashes me a snaggletoothed grin, steps backward off the platform, and plummets to the ground.

The faint whirring sound of his pulley speeding along the rope is my only clue that he is alive before he pops into view again, a hundred feet away, spinning playfully as he careens into the trees and out of view.

"I thought you were the safety instructor!" I yell after him.

"I'm not the safety instructor!" call the trees. "I'm a risk mitigator."

"Risk mitigator," I grumble, locking in my carabiner as I prepare for my first line. I sit back into my harness and will my fingers to let go. "Let go, Kate," I say quietly, embarrassed. "Please let go." My pinky wiggles a little, and nothing else.

"Can I help, honey?" calls Katherine, but she is attached to a tree off to the side of the platform. For safety. Or, rather, risk mitigation.

"I'm great!" I reply, hugging the platform tightly. "Everything is normal."

I stand there for a minute, maybe two, maybe five. The birds chirp, and I contemplate shooting them from the sky.

The wholesome face of the second guide appears beside me, smiling.

"Hello, again," she says. "Are you feeling okay?"

"Yes," I reply in an unnaturally chirpy voice. "It's just that . . . I have been almost dying recently." I look down a few hundred feet below my own and try to wriggle my toes. Nothing.

"Ahhh. I see," she says.

I glance at the forest fluttering around me, thick with chestnut oaks, white pine, and hickories, and realize that I had never considered how much I hate trees.

"I . . . um . . . spend a lot of time trying not to die. So I can't tell if I'm being reasonable right now."

"Fear feels the same," she says gently.

"Yes, exactly," I say. "So maybe I should just stay here."

"You can do that. No problem. We will have to find our way down, one way or another. But I understand. I had a similar feeling." She trails off the way Southern women do when they are inviting intimacy.

"You did?"

"I did," she says, leaning precariously over the edge of the platform beside me as she explains that she had to have one of her lungs removed in her early twenties.

It was only a couple years ago, but she has been testing her limits ever since by taking up adventure guiding and running, and, this last year, she completed a whole marathon. By the time she is done, we are seated comfortably, dangling in the air and my hand is loosely gripping the rope above me.

"Everything is a risk. There is something kind of wonderful about being afraid when you remember that not all risks are equal," she says.

Maybe it's the altitude or the fact that she is my only way down, but I think she's right.

It takes great courage to live. Period. There are fears and disappointments and failures every day, and, in the end, the hero dies. It must be cinematic to watch us from above.

"Are you ready to take some mitigated risk?" I yell to no one in particular.

"Ready," says Katherine.

"Set," says the guide.

"Go," I say more to myself, because I am gone.

———

CHAPTER SIX

Do What You Love (and the Money Will Follow)

I AM INCURABLE. I HAVE A DURABLE ILLNESS. Toban and I are holding words up to the light like gemstones.

In the last few months, the immunotherapy has been wonderfully successful in fighting the cancer without the aid of chemotherapy, and each tumor is now a fraction of its original size. Still, they remain, holding steady, the subject of endless debate. The field of oncology is not clear about what to do next with a rare patient like me. Are these remaining lesions dead or dormant? This cancer could kill me or leave me alone. How afraid should I be? Every oncologist I

contact seems to have a different theory, but, no matter how many times I inquire, Dr. Cartwright is resis-
tant to asking others for their advice. As a fellow
university professor, I find it impossible to understand
his reasoning. *Aren't you curious? Shouldn't we gather
the prevailing opinions?* My life is in the balance.

I may not have much time before the cancer begins
to grow again, so any surgical attempt at a cure must
happen now. Unwilling to let Dr. Cartwright's strange
reluctance deter me, I ask a few of my historian
friends—all wonderful researchers—to help me hear
more from the brightest minds. Almost immediately
they create an online database with research so
sprawling that the project earns its own nickname:
No Kate Left Behind, referring both to a bygone
Bush-era educational policy and to the odd fact that
all of us are named Kate. My Kates ask everyone:
How are other patients like her faring? What is your
opinion on surgery? What are the short-term survival
rates?

According to most, I will have to take a highly ambitious approach. One particularly menacing tumor is
buried deep in my liver near a rich cord carrying the
blood from the lower half of my body. Nick it and I

will bleed out on the operating table. Only a world-class surgeon could dig it out and leave me cancer-free.

"I wouldn't recommend it though," advises one such world-class surgeon. "I would be leaving you with only a tiny fragment of your liver." I am driving, and he has called me after a long day because he is merciful and knows the window for me to make this decision is short.

"How much liver could you leave me?"

"Certainly less than twenty percent, depending on the exact placement of the tumor. But a radical hepa-tectomy would also change your life significantly. You'd be prone to infections and fatigue. This is not in the same category as the other liver resections you are considering. You would have a diminished life with a high probability of liver failure."

Diminished life. I think he was reaching for dimin-ished *quality of life*, but we are settling on something that rings truer. I would be cured and dying.

The surgeon pauses. We are quietly working through this word problem: Kate has 100 percent of her liver, but 30 percent is riddled with cancer. The cancer is scattered. How much cancer can be removed if having less than 20 percent of her liver will kill Kate?

But the blood feels like it is rushing from my head now and my decision to take this call while driving home from giving a lecture about the history of Quakerism is seeming increasingly stupid. I pull the car over to the shoulder of this country road.

"What is liver failure like?" I ask finally, trying to keep my voice steady.

"It's slow, Kate. It's really slow. Your belly swells and your skin yellows when your liver can't fully digest food. Fluids build up and create pressure on the diaphragm. You'll struggle to breathe while the toxins build up in your system and reduce your ability to think. It's . . . slow."

"Months, I suppose."

"Months," he agrees.

"Sorry for the oversimplification, but if I want a cure then you're saying I can risk death on the operating table and, if I survive, die slowly of liver failure?"

"Yes. And even if you don't die of liver failure, your quality of life will be significantly reduced. That's your best-case scenario."

The sky is churning with steely clouds and soon rain is pattering against the windshield. I kill the ignition and ease my head against the top of the steering wheel.

"I really appreciate you calling, doctor." I sound far away, even to myself. "If you don't mind, I'll get a few other opinions and get back to you soon about whether to schedule a surgery date."

I hang up the phone and close my eyes. Sharp inhale, fast exhale, I try to ease myself back into breath but my mind is a tight circle. *There is no way out.* I try to set a rhythm—in through the nose, out through the mouth—until I can hear the rain slowing to a spit. I turn on the engine, ready to ease the car back onto the highway, but the grass around the car tires is soft and swollen, bloated with everything that refuses to be washed away.

THERE IS AN ITCHY feeling I get when I am still. I am from Winnipeg, which floats like an island on the prairies, and that much open space makes you want to do something like alphabetize your father's vast library against his will. *A* is for almanacs that gave me my first glimpses of a sexual education until my mom left a book on my pillow called *Preparing for Adolescence,* which I read and then dutifully filed under *G* for gross.

Then, somewhere in the mix of high school and

college, I got hooked on the feeling of trying, the strain of pushing against something impossibly heavy and wondering if it would budge. Though I quickly intuited that the word *ambitious* was not a compliment for a woman, I took my dad's advice: the key to ambition was being willing to keep your bum in a chair for an extremely long period of time. By that measure, I was enormously ambitious.

The first time my father saw the full fruits of this labor—a splendid office on Duke University's sumptuous green campus—he said, affectionately, "If you ever leave a place like this, I'll murder you."

But now I worry that I climbed too high, too fast, only to be dangling from a branch. There is nothing here in this beautiful university but more to do.

When I opened the door to my office for the first time in months, I immediately yelled down the hall for my friend Will to come over. Will is a bishop, professor, and the only person to use a Sunday sermon to make fun of me in front of a bustling congregation, so I tend to come to him with my failures before he discovers them later.

"Will, look at this." I look directly at the hundreds upon hundreds of books lining my walls. Each shelf is elegantly organized by historical era and ornamented with enough knickknacks to suggest a deep acquaintance with the period. For academics, bookshelves are trophy cases. *Behold all the ideas I have conquered! Don't touch! It's really quite a rare edition.*

"What am I looking at?" he says, scanning the room.

"This!" I gesture like an irate Vanna White. "This! Just *look at this.*"

Will peers at the books more closely. "I see a lot of books about the history of American religion. But you *teach* the history of American religion."

"Do you think that I intended to read fifty books about Puritan dietary customs?"

"We have a high tolerance for obscurity," he says with a laugh.

"I don't know how this got so out of control. My friend's husband died in his medical residency after working over a decade to be a doctor, and I can't stop thinking about it. We start paying into these careers. We start and we think, how much could it possibly cost?"

"Are you asking me?"

"Yes."

"Wait, are you back? Are you teaching again? I thought you were still on medical leave."

"I'm tired of medical leave."

Bishop Will considers this for a moment.

"Are you sure you should push through? No one would blame you for focusing on your treatment right now."

"No one tells you that fear is extremely boring. And I miss work," I say, sitting down heavily on the couch. He arranges himself next to me and we contemplate the bookshelf in silence.

"Will?"

"Hmmmm?" His eyes are closed, his arms are crossed and his shoulders slumped, a sure sign that he is turning over ideas for a new sermon.

"How will I know when this work has cost me too much?"

"Hmmmmmmmm," he answers, squinting his eyes a little more. "It likely depends on whether this is a career or a calling."

WHEN I GOT MY first real job at Duke University, an administrator sat me down with a stack of papers and informed me that I needed to accomplish ten things in seven years in order to keep my employment. I would have to write two weighty books of original research and eight scholarly articles, at which point my superiors in the greater university would sit down to deliberate my intellectual merit. Then and only then could I live at my own pace.

Somewhere in those years a woman in this line of work has to figure out if she has time to be pregnant and raise a family. That was not entirely clear to me until I found a wonderful cohort of American religion scholars my age and discovered that every man had three children and every woman had one or none. Women in academia simply didn't have the time to be simultaneously biologically and intellectually productive. If we wanted children, we had to set our biological watches to what was appropriately called "the tenure clock." When the tenure alarm sounded, 2,550 days after signing on the dotted line at Duke University, I would need to have established myself as a leading scholar and prodigious writer with an undisputed specialty. And all I felt was a mixture of fear and appreciation for the chance to scramble to keep a job that had eluded my father my entire life.

MY FATHER LEFT THE house when I was fourteen. He did not leave me and my sisters, nor would anyone in their right mind have abandoned a wife who was a dead ringer for Diane Lane. But he was gone, and we had helped him pack his meager collection of clothes—five shirts, one blazer, two sweaters and one pair of navy slacks—into a floppy suitcase and scoured the house for anything else he might need. Most of the weight in his luggage was books, which we asked him to reconsider. We could keep them until he was ready, whenever that was.

It was in our family bathroom, dusty rose wallpaper peeling from the humidity, that I took inventory of his absence: his razor, toothbrush, and a wide-tooth comb for his hair, copper as a handful of pennies. He left one of his dozen pairs of reading glasses beside the tub because he deemed it perfectly natural for a bathroom to have a fully stocked library, which I deemed to be wildly unsanitary. My mom would regularly leave him notes to replace the toilet paper roll (*You can do it! Yes, you can!*), but he was much more invested in a well-stocked mind.

Both my parents had, in their twenties, done what no one in their families had ever accomplished and gone to college, where, for some reason, they made quite a show of it. Both received scholarships at English universities to pursue their doctoral degrees, my father in history and my mother in music. My dad was a spark plug who loved cricket, Tudor history, and keeping two toddlers from getting concussions (with mixed results) in a tiny apartment up eight flights of stairs. My mother had a spectacular mezzo-soprano voice and performed around Europe in an avant-garde singing group called Electric Phoenix, whose greatest hits sounded like classically trained ghosts haunting what was left of the disco era. She even met Prince Charles. Twice.

When they decided to move back to Canada to find employment, jobs were sparse. They followed the faint trail of university work until it led the family to the University of Manitoba. There my mom shone, later becoming the first woman with a doctorate to be tenured at their school of music.

When my sisters and I were too sick for school, we would nap in my mother's office under her maple-wood piano or run shrieking through the hallways to hear the acoustics made by three girls high on orange soda. We rarely visited my father, who was housed in an honest-to-God storage closet in a building that caused us all to wonder why the university had financed its own renaissance in Stalinist architecture. He was an *adjunct* faculty member, a Latin term meaning *subordinate,* and was treated as such. Every few months, he was expected to reapply for his job, if he hoped to work again the following semester. Or find himself applying for unemployment insurance again. Most of my childhood memories of my father were of him sitting at a desk buried under stacks of thin blue exam books that he graded hundreds at a time.

He could only patch an income together by racing between three separate universities every week, teaching any class deemed undesirable by the permanent faculty. So he mastered topics ranging from Medieval English crime to Canadian colonialism to the history of Bart Simpson. It was a ludicrous schedule by any standard. He had spent a decade preparing, not for a career, but for entrance into a guild of scholars, only to be pumping quarters into the campus soda machine at 2:00 A.M. for another Diet Mountain Dew. He slipped further and further from us, sleeping later, growing heavier, and rumbling with a kind of anger that I could not have named until I saw it in myself: outrage and fear that everything he'd done would amount to nothing.

This lasted for a decade. I was fourteen years old when my dad was offered the chance to have a full-time job with lovely colleagues and his name on the door and his own research center. It was two provinces away in Calgary at a school where I had once won a jelly-bean-eating competition. There he became unrecognizable to me. He was now a man who threw Tupperware parties for students, and who coached a hockey team so he could lead chants of genteel derision at rival teams and bad referees ("We Beg to Differ! We Beg to Differ! Shabby! Shabby!"). From the bottom of our Bowler family hearts, we believed that this job saved his life.

But, as I am learning from a diagram of my liver, everything costs something.

Doctors have taken a sliver of my tumor and placed it in a lab rat to see how he would fare. The rat and I are both subjects in someone's study, but no one will tell me how the little animal is doing. Are we okay?

"Even waiting is going to take its toll," says a doctor at my twelfth consultation. I drove a long way to see her, and I am sitting on her examining table in a hospital gown, swinging my bare legs. "Given how often we are putting you in an MRI machine . . ."

"What do you mean?" I ask. "Because my cancer is always growing?"

"No," she says glumly. "We are screening you for

cancer so frequently that I'm worried that we are going to cause *new* cancer."

At which point I openly roll my eyes and start pulling on my pants.

TEQUILA IS NOT PERMITTED on the campus of Regent University, the stomping grounds of televangelist and conservative icon Pat Robertson, so T.J., Doug, and I have found a restaurant nearby with some thoroughly acceptable chips and guacamole to soften the blow of margaritas. I drove the four hours from Durham to Virginia Beach, Virginia, on the weekend, between chemotherapy appointments, because this is what we do. Professors, sequestered in universities and colleges around the country, preserve our most precious intellectual friendships by signing up to give free lectures at conferences absolutely anywhere in order to argue with other professors through the night with a specificity that curls the toes of our loved ones. No detail too specific. No comment too pretentious. We are mentally sprinting and stopping and stretching and laughing while cutting one another off.

T.J. and Doug coaxed me into giving a lecture on the research project I had started before my diagnosis, a modern history of conservative Christian women. But that feeling of intellectual possibility and mastery is floating further and further afield.

"What are you going to do with that lecture, Bowler?" T.J. asks, smiling at the waitress with a gesture that says, *Yes, another pitcher of margaritas.*

The night is growing deeper, and now that most of our intellectual wrangling about the history of evangelicalism has been set aside, I can feel them beginning to tug at the threads of my work.

"How much archival research do you have left to do?" queries Doug.

T.J. and I exchange looks, and I stifle a nervous laugh. Doug is legendary in our group for deep dives into the archives, and he is nearing completion of an epic history of religious revivals that captivated the Protestant world in the eighteenth century. By comparison, my work feels too small, too rough-hewn, to be building up to anything.

"I don't know," I begin, trying to focus and give an honest account. "I had done a lot before, I guess."

"How far did you get?" he asks, and my friends settle back in their chairs as if to say, *Start from the beginning.*

So I begin to tell them about heaps of dates and

interviews and maps. Hundreds of hours of footage of conferences and sermons. A massive database I had built to track if and how women are allowed to lead in the largest American churches. I had been showing up at events and, to date, had interviewed over a hundred Christian celebrities and supporting industry leaders. I glance at the clock on the wall and realize I've been prattling on for the better part of an hour, but both men are still nodding as if filing each fact in a drawer.

"But that feels a bit silly right now," I say, trailing off.

"Why silly?" T.J. asks, concerned. He would have made a great psychologist.

"Well, it's all just a bit . . ."

"What?" T.J's voice is firm but kind. "What is this?" He makes a sweeping motion like he is splaying it out, all the obsessive reading and searching and mulling and writing we've been talking about for hours now.

"I don't know . . . It's feeling a little ridiculous lately," I say, not sounding nearly as philosophical as I'd intended. It took my father a decade to write his history of Christmas. It took me ten years to write my last book on the history of the prosperity gospel. And I am only guaranteed eight months more. "It costs us *everything* to do this work and, right now, I'm really wondering: what is the point?"

At heart, professors are petty romantics. We have fallen in love with the smell of old books and the thrill of discovering a nugget of gold in a pile of intellectual excrement. We teach and write and ruin family holidays with the hope that sound scholarship helps bear up the weight of civilization; but, in practice, we spend most of our intellectual lives chasing gainful employment, trying to sell more than five hundred copies of a book that took us eight years to write, and protesting the promotion of our colleagues on the grounds that they did not give enough praise to our last book. We will love this career long after it breaks our hearts.

"Well . . ." T.J. looks around for a moment and then smiles broadly as another pitcher of margaritas arrives on the table. He gives me a moment to settle by taking his time pouring us each another one, and stops for a moment more for a swig and a lick of salt.

"Look, Bowler," he says finally. "I saw you today up at the front. You had everyone absolutely spellbound. *No.* Hear me. This is *who you are*."

I stare back at him dolefully.

"Write the book," he says firmly.

"But what if I die this summer . . ." I am pouring out the coldest words now, dug from the bottom of the well. "My final moments on the planet will be spent writing a stupid historical book that no one will read—all for a job I can't keep—when I should have spent every precious minute with my son, who won't remember me anyway."

This strange dream, my father's dream. It's time to let it go.

Doug has been silent for some time, his hands folded on the table and index fingers pressed together like a steeple. He taps them together a few times as if settling on a thought, then he looks up to give me the full weight of his mind.

"Kate, I don't doubt that you will find a way to focus most of your attention on your son. You've always done that, and you'll continue to do that. But the way you're framing your work . . . it's not quite right. In my opinion."

He pauses. "Do you love this work?"

"Yes," I confess.

"And you're wonderful at it." He does not ask this as a question. "But you keep framing your relationships as the only thing of value as if work is somehow secondary or simply an expression of your ambitions and desires. But this is what you love and where your gifts lie and . . . I don't know how to say this except directly."

I try to look at him, but I am flooded with emotion.

"Kate," he tries again, "if the worst happens and this book is the last thing you ever do, Zach can still find you there."

T.J. puts his hand on my back as I bury my face in my hands.

"You're in there, Bowler. So write the book," T.J. agrees.

"Okay," I say, clearing my throat with embarrassment. "Yup. Okay then." I wave at the waitress who is doing an excellent job pretending our table is not in the midst of a wake. "Thanks, ma'am. Yes. We've got more to discuss. We're going to need another round."

The next morning, I skip the conference altogether, head across campus and swing open a set of heavy library doors.

The student worker behind the long counter is on his phone, zoned out in this vast uninterrupted maze of shelves, without another person in sight.

"Hello!" I say, cheerily. "I checked your databases this morning, and I see that you have all forty years of this magazine." I hand him a slip of paper with the call number. "I'll need your help scanning. Can I show you what I mean?" And I am off.

The student trails after me as I zip up and through the stacks, nimbly interpreting the signs though I've never been here before. Soon we are standing before two full walls of glossy magazines looking woefully undisturbed.

"I'll start at the scanner first? I'll let you label the files," I chirp.

"Which magazine?" asks the young man wearily.

I am barely able to mask my enthusiasm.

"All of them."

WE HAVE GONE OVER it again. My doctor friend, Max, is over and we are walking through the dozens of small judgments that are leading me to this decision. We talk about "debulking cancer" and the risks inherent in resection. We discuss the future of immunotherapy and whether a second drug might come along in time. He helps me turn the details over and over until the language and choices feel familiar.

"I think I'd like to have the entire right lobe of the liver resected. That's over half of the organ, but it will grow back. Sorry, it will *hypertrophy*. Not grow back.

But that would remove a couple of the larger tumors and we can revisit the inoperable one with radiation afterward."

"Okay," Max says finally, "then here we are."

"Here we are," I echo, tucking the blanket around my feet. No matter the temperature, I insist that all impossible decisions must be made outside under the uninterrupted sky. How else could you know that you're still alive?

"Then here's something I do with my patients. I tell them to mark the date. You've made a decision based on all the information you have right now. Next week there might be a new treatment or a new setback and all the reasons why you chose this might seem obsolete. You could drive yourself crazy wondering *What if* or *I should have* . . . But right now, in this moment, you know that this is the best you can do with the information you have."

"You have to give yourself the gift of saying 'I couldn't have known . . . ' " I repeat.

"Exactly," he says. "This decision, like all decisions, must stand *in time,* for better or for worse."

I ease myself back on the bench to get a better view of the clouds sifting shades of blue.

"Then here we are."

"Here we are," Max agrees, "on a Wednesday."

WHEN, THREE YEARS AFTER leaving, my father moved back home from the good university job in Calgary, I had already left for college, but I knew he was different. He'd come back to the same Stalinist buildings in Manitoba. Same minuscule pay. Same collegial loneliness. But shouldn't *someone,* he insisted, be writing a vast encyclopedia of Christmas and perhaps a companion volume about the history of Santa Claus himself?

The University of Manitoba is renegotiating the adjunct-faculty contracts once again, and word has come down that my elderly father will need to teach more classes with even less job security and, all at once, he knows in his bones that this is no longer a calling. It is simply work.

"Well, that's it I guess," says my father to one of the last classes he will ever teach. "I look at the calendar and there is not enough time left to learn Chinese. I always wanted to learn Chinese. And what is the difference between rap and hip-hop?"

My mom reports that the students laughed but that Dad had that pinchy expression he gets when he can't entirely land on a thought.

"I've heard people say that life is like a roll of toilet paper: the closer you get to the end, the faster it goes. That seems truer now . . ." says my father, before sharply returning to a historical lesson about the many deficiencies of the French.

The next day, when he goes to collect his things from his office, he almost trips over a stack of toilet paper sitting outside of his door.

He picks up a roll and it unwinds to the floor, scrawled with blue ink. It is the definition of rap versus hip-hop. It is a rudimentary lesson in Chinese characters. And the students had written a friendly admonition: *Slow down. There's still plenty of time.*

"So I think that's what I'll do," he tells me over the phone later that night. "I'll stop speeding toward the end. What else is there for me to do?"

"I don't understand, Dad," I press him. "You made your peace with university life years ago. I'm not saying you should sign the crappy new contract, but I don't get it. I thought you were throwing pearls before swine."

Pearls before swine, sweetie.

He had said it all my life. At the dinner table. In the car. Before my elementary school presentation about Mozart to a class who wanted to hear a kid named Tyler talk about Mötley Crüe. I could hear my dad saying, *Knowledge is knowledge. Do it regardless.* Pearls before Tylers.

"I did love teaching," he says slowly. "But now . . . I think . . . it's always permissible to hope for more."

"Well then," I say, after a pause. "That sounds extremely reasonable."

"It does, doesn't it?"

"Oh, news. I've decided to finish my book. I've got five more months before the tenure clock runs out. So I've run the math, and I would have to write 500 perfect words for the remaining 183 days to finish a manuscript that's 100,000 words long," I say breathlessly.

It's absurd, and we both know it.

"That sounds splendid," he says grandly. "I'll follow your career with interest."

THE NEXT FEW MONTHS are a blur of early-morning writing sprees, long afternoons at the hospital, and hours in between with a small boy and a puppet named Mr. Walrus, who helps him tidy up after it appears that a velociraptor has terrorized our home. Every night my father carefully reads my work, makes suggestions, and declares today's labors to be "quite acceptable."

Five months after I began, the day before my tenure dossier is due, I shoot him the entire manuscript so he can read the dedication tucked between the title and the preface.

> *For Dad*
> *who dusted me off and sent me back up the*
> *mountain after I fell all the way down.*

He stares at the screen and blinks back what appears to be a sudden onslaught of allergies.

"Well," he grunts, "you didn't fall very far."

"Thank you, Dad," I say quietly. "This was a very good dream."

"It was, wasn't it?" agrees my father, sitting back in his chair and folding his hands over his stomach. "Very good indeed."

—

THE FAMILY IS BUZZING again, this time over my liver resection. My mother-in-law is packing up Zach's pajamas, shorts, shirts, and swimming trunks, along with seventeen stuffed animals that—after mashing them against his face, inhaling, and sighing bliss-fully—he has deemed necessary companions. My in-laws have mercifully volunteered to spirit him away for a little vacation the moment they know I am safely through surgery, because I can't bear the thought of him seeing me in the hospital.

I know how little there is for me to pack—face wash, toothbrush, wide-mouth socks, and a hairbrush—because the bulk of the work is mental. Smile at the hospital intake coordinator. Braid my hair and tuck it into the surgical cap. Don't worry about the knots, this gown is coming off anyway. Show the nurse which veins didn't work last time for the intravenous needle. Accept the feeling of light hysteria the mo-ment the stretcher lurches into motion toward the op-erating theater.

The staff will give you a moment if you stretch out your hand to the old man in the clerical collar waiting by the doorway. Family and friends have been swept into the waiting room with assurances and a pager, but he has been waiting for this moment because he knows what must be done. His calling has prepared him for it.

"It's four A.M., Will," I croak. "You must really love me."

The bishop ignores this, as Southern gentlemen do. He moves to the front of the gurney to rest a hand on my head.

"Lord Jesus, bless these surgeons and the work of their hands. Bless her care and her healing. And bless this precious daughter of yours."

I stare up at him, blinking tears, but his eyes are squeezed tight.

"God, if you please, keep this one alive. Her best work is yet to come."

CHAPTER SEVEN

———

Apocalyptic Time

THE MEETING LASTED ONLY TEN MINUTES BE-
cause I couldn't think of much to say. If there had
been a video camera in the examining room that day,
it would have recorded a series of utterly unremarkable motions. A doctor comes in and shakes hands
with the patient. The patient nods while the doctor is
speaking. The computer monitor at the desk is flicked
on so the doctor can show the patient a series of
black-and-white images. The patient readjusts her
chair to get a better view as the doctor points at the
screen. The doctor shrugs. The patient shrugs. There
is a brief exchange of words, a business card is handed

over, and the patient puts it in her backpack. Both exit.

I HAD SPENT A sluggish summer after the liver resection tending to the seven-inch incision bisecting my abdomen. Surgery is an act of exquisitely restrained violence, and recovery is the strange aftermath. Did this really happen to me? This can't be my body. Give me a minute here to check. Nope. This must belong to someone else.

"I miss holding Zach," I told Toban wistfully on our nightly shuffle around the block. "He's like a basket of puppies."

"This is a bit more like a basket full of Dobermans," Toban replied, picking up Zach and throwing him over his shoulder to delighted screams.

I was set to meet with the radiation oncology team to talk about targeting the most dangerous tumor that could not be cut out.

I had been waiting almost two hours by the time the radiation oncologist came into the examining room and shook my hand. "I'm sorry," she said, a little winded. "But I couldn't find it.

"I couldn't find it at *all*," she said again, stretching

out the last word as she booted up the computer. "I'll show you. We had to get the whole team together to look for it."

The images were familiar to me at this point, the white column of my spine, the grainy outlines of my lungs, kidneys, and liver swimming in and out of view as the doctor searched for the right angle of vision. There was a strange dark cavity where an entire lobe of my liver once was and fresh tissue was impressively swelling to fill the void.

"Ah, here it is." She rested on an image.

"Again, sorry for the delay. I assembled the radiology team to confirm what I was seeing. It took us forever to figure out where it went, but it's here." She had drawn a line in lime green, as short and thin as a dime.

We both leaned forward toward the screen, cocking our heads to the side. My stomach lurched. The remaining marble-sized tumor had disappeared. I had always been told that the best-case scenario was that these tumors would be dead or dormant, but never gone.

"Why is it gone?" I asked quietly.

"Maybe it got squished . . . like a pancake?" Her voice climbed an octave, as if reaching for the conclusion.

"What would squish a tumor?" I asked. "Is this related to the surgery?"

"I don't think so, no," she replied. We can't take our eyes off the screen.

"My last tumor is . . . squished," I repeated.

"I believe so."

"Then . . ."

"We can scan again in October if you want," she offered, "but I wouldn't radiate this."

"Okay," I said. "I'll have to think about that."

"I should probably write this down for you," she said brightly, perhaps sensing that I was not in any position to think clearly. She took out her business card and wrote down the kind of radiation she would have used to treat it. Then she wrote *pancake tumor* in blue-inked cursive at the bottom.

"So that's what happened today," she said, handing me the card.

"Right. Thank you," I said, putting it in the pocket of my backpack and heading out the door.

I tell Toban about the pancake tumor and then—after the news causes him to close his eyes, rub his temples, then go take a nap—no one else. There is nothing casual about our language now, nothing held lightly or ventured without evidence. We don't use words that might have to be unsaid, or run back to hopes we've laid aside. There is a fellowship among the afflicted, and it is marked by silence.

I patiently waited another two weeks for my oncology appointment, and then the ten minutes it took for Dr. Cartwright to find the bright green line that the radiation oncologist had drawn onto the scan.

"Yeah, that's gone," he said.

"It's not just squished?" I asked hopefully.

"It's gone," he repeated.

I had been asking doctors across the country if they had patients with a "complete response" to immunotherapy, but I had only heard of a handful of cases.

"Okay," I said softly, a smile spreading over my face as he clicked closed the bright images and turned the monitor to black.

MOST OF MY FAMILY and friends accept the news of my disappearing tumor wholeheartedly, as if it is something they had already believed. *She's cured. Praise God. It's a miracle.* They chew through the facts a little, their voices light with wonder, and then suddenly we are back to talking about soccer practice and what toppings are on the pizza in the oven. It's over. But the truth is, for most people, this was over long ago.

It is a strange fact that sometimes the people who love you most will be among the first to stop worrying about you. An inflexible optimism stands as a barrier between you. *You will be fine.* Anything to the contrary seems too difficult to communicate. Pain is simultaneously intimate and distant, intense and boring. And, according to my rough calculations, any news, no matter how terrible, seems like old hat after about three months. *Your leg spontaneously exploded? The polar bears are unionizing now? Oh, I heard that already.*

We find it especially difficult to talk about anything chronic—meaning any kind of pain, emotional or physical, that abides and lives with us constantly. The sustaining myth of the American Dream rests on a hearty can-do spirit surmounting all obstacles, but not all problems can be overcome. So often we are defined by the troubles we live with, rather than the things we conquer. Any persistent suffering requires being afraid, but who can stay awake to fear for so long?

My friend Luke once told me that the Christian

tradition has special language for our three experiences of time: tragic, apocalyptic, and pastoral.

"What you are describing right now is tragic time," he said. Tragic time is the grand theodicy. The problem of evil has swept away the illusion that all things will be made right, and suddenly we wonder at the goodness of the world. We grapple with the simultaneous length and brevity of our existence. We are Heathcliff, forced to lose our Catherines and endure our storied life as a collection of memorabilia that we have loved and lost.

"You are excellent at that kind of time," he said generously, because I am.

I grinned.

"But then there is apocalyptic time. Which is related, but not identical." The veil has been lifted and now we see ourselves on the brink. Systems are irredeemably broken and injustice reigns. The word *apocalypse* translates to *revelation,* and its prophets look to different signs. Some see supernatural clues, sins that have pushed the nation off its moral axis or kept communities from bringing God's kingdom to earth. And now we must retreat to the hills, purge our impurities, restore Israel, or keep watch for the Antichrist. Most apocalypticists need only look to the planet itself. Only a few degrees keep the ice caps from melting and the brush fires from raging and the soil from turning fetid from our poisons. The end of the world is nigh.

There is a wonderful and terrible clarity to apocalyptic time. The last chapter has been read, and, now that it is too late, all the hidden facets of our stories are beginning to reveal themselves. The people we saw begging through the car window, the acquaintances we made and then forgot, the friends whose burdens or privileges became too exhausting or alienating. There was a Great Drama all along, in which our tender humanity, our worried hopes, were all interwoven. I keep bumping into this realization again and again as if for the first time: we were always the same.

I could see this clearly in the early-Wednesday-morning hours in the Atlanta airport when I used to visit the homeless moms with young children in the bathroom, washing their kids' sleepy faces in the sink and hoping to find a way to get them to school. They would sleep near the baggage carousel with a suitcase of all their things, pretending to be waiting for a flight. How had I not seen the world as it really is? Now nothing can tear these scenes from my mind.

I know I am meant to be comforted by the Christian belief in a redemptive apocalypse—a sudden and wonderful conclusion is coming, a burst of blinding light that will sear our eyes and fill our hearts with terror and relief. But in the meantime, *screw this*. If this is the very end of my existence, do I want to be here . . . answering email? In moments like that, I have been known to rent bulldozers, leave without warning in the middle of professional lunches, and give away essential furniture on Facebook until my husband politely asks, in the comments, for his favorite chair to be kept.

Most people, if they have any choice in the matter, will choose neither apocalyptic nor tragic time. They live in pastoral time, Luke explains. Pastoral time is marked by the seasons, the sowing and reaping and herding that keeps the land tilled and the herds fenced. We are reminded why the title *pastor* comes from the word *shepherd*, because most of Christian ministry will be spent attending to everyday life. My students at the divinity school sign up for the grand cause of joining God in bringing heaven to earth but mostly find themselves fiddling with the sanctuary sound system and trying to get what's-her-face off the church council.

"It sounds extremely boring," I interrupt.

"The church calendar calls it Ordinary Time, Kate, and it is *most of life*," he says, fixing me with a look. Englishmen are wonderful at these pointed moments, committed as they are to devastating restraint.

"Fine," I concede. "I guess I'm not used to it anymore."

Hadn't I become a little smug? A little too sure that the drama of the world's end was always more important than groceries and hanging photos and paying taxes? There must be a time for everything.

We receive news that Toban's beloved grandmother has died, so we pile onto a plane and return home to Manitoba. Hundreds of well-wishers fill up Grandma's rural church to say goodbye and listen to her husband and children tell stories, read scripture, and sing in elegant harmonies. Long ago, Mennonites made a satanic pact in exchange for the gift of song but no one wants to discuss this theory with me at the moment. After the service, elderly ladies fill buffet tables with buns and marshmallow salads and any recipe they can scale by a hundred (which is to say, everything), and later the family meets to have our own graveside service to see her laid to rest next to the farm where she spent her eight decades. The coffin is open and she lies peacefully under the October sun.

We cry and hold hands while the grandkids ruin their funeral clothes by climbing all over the nearby hay bales.

The crops have been harvested so the fields are spare, and the family looks so beautiful standing there, restless with love. Before we leave for North Carolina, I make my own plans accordingly. I buy plots of land for our own graves near the edge of the farm because, someday long in the future, we will sleep together under the snow as another grandson mends the wooden fence next to the barley.

THE SURGEON POINTS AT a dark blob on the monitor, flitting through bright images as he taps the screen with his pen. There it is. You can see its depth better from this angle. Here it is again from the side.

He was supposed to examine the long strip bisecting my abdomen, admiring the way his incisions had closed without puckering. He would show me the results of my new scans, pointing to the shadowy cavity where a pound of liver had been extracted. We would shake hands. *I didn't get a chance to thank you before. You did an excellent job with the procedure.*

Instead I stare dumbly at an image of an obvious

tumor. Something new has grown inside me. Something that no one said could happen. It looks like an aggressive cancer. The surgeon shifts his weight on the stool and clears his throat, pausing for me to catch up. *This was a follow-up. This was just a follow-up.*

The surgeon seems to decide against waiting any further for me to speak and excuses himself. Eventually he returns with some paperwork. Dr. Cartwright can't join us, he reports, but he has been consulted about the next steps. I've been scheduled for radiation again somewhere in the bowels of the hospital. He wishes me the very best.

The surgeon closes the door behind him.

Someone knocks softly and the intake nurse pops her head in.

"Did you bring anyone with you, dear?" she asks gently.

"Oh, no . . . it was just a follow-up," I explain. But there are no explanations.

DURING THESE LONG DAYS I am preparing for Zach's fourth birthday, and bedtimes are lengthy re-enactments of the day he was born. To my great credit, I have managed to remove all the gory and painful bits and distill the story to its central plotline: the great discovery.

"When I had a baby in my tummy, I knew one day that he was trying to get out. And the baby pushed and pushed. And do you know who that was?" I ask.

"It was me!" he exclaims gleefully. He knows his lines.

"But I didn't know that yet," I say. "So I went to the hospital. And this baby pushed and pushed, but he wouldn't come out."

"It was me!"

"But I didn't know that yet.

"Finally, it was time. The baby pushed and pushed and *finally* he arrived. The nurses picked him up and wiped him off and checked him and weighed him . . ." By this point, he can hardly stand the suspense.

"It was me, Mom!"

"Well, finally, the nurse put the baby in my arms. The baby and I looked into each other's eyes for the first time, and we loved each other. We loved each other that very moment. And you know what I said?" His eyes are wide. This is our favorite part, so we take our time.

"I said, 'It was *you*. It was *you* the whole time.' "

"It was me," he says. And sighs. "And that's how I

was borned? And then I get bigger and bigger? And you were a baby? And you got bigger?" He has been stuck on the question of how people age. "But Grandma is buried," he says suddenly. "They dug a big, big hole. And they put that lady in the dirt."

"Oh, love. Great-grandma was really special. When she died, everyone was really sad and they put her body in the ground. But we think that her spirit—the part that made Grandma special—went into heaven to be with God. That's why we were sad and also happy, because we think we will see her again."

He is silent, looking around his room.

"But moms do not get buried," he says sharply. It is a question as much as a demand.

"Oh, no, sweetie," I say too quickly. I am not ready.

"Moms do not get buried," he repeats, his eyes boring into mine.

"Normally, people get old before they die," I finish uncertainly.

"And then they be with God?" he says.

"Yes."

"But I can't see God."

"Sometimes we feel God here," I say, putting my hand on his small chest. "If we are lucky, we see God in something really mysterious, like a miracle. But mostly we see God in regular surprises like love and forgiveness."

"I think Great-grandma is buried in the backyard," he says finally. "We can dig for her and find her."

"Great-grandma is buried in Canada, sweetie. And even if we dig and we find her, she won't wake up."

Zach closes his eyes for a long minute. "Then lie down with me, Mom."

As I slip in beside him, blinking back tears, I am reminded of my friend Bishop Will when he was preparing to preside over the funeral of a small boy. He took a deep breath and steadied himself to walk out and face down the grieving parents. But then he paused, and suddenly looked up to the sky.

"God, don't you make me go out there and lie for you again," he hissed.

I TELL MY FRIENDS and family, gently. There is none of the drama this time. There will be no racing to the airport or tearful declarations. We are realists now.

I'll begin radiation in two weeks. Unsure of what to do, the next day I numbly follow the travel plans I had made months ago to fly sixteen long hours to north-ern Alberta. There I'll give a lecture at the university where my Mennonite friend Joe is a professor and then come straight home for Zach's fourth birthday.

"You should have canceled," says Joe, hugging me outside the airport. "We would have understood." I shrug, embarrassed and puffy-eyed. He takes the lug-gage from my hands and carefully places it in the trunk of his car.

"You must be overwhelmed," he continues, watch-ing me with concern. I feel ragged, hanging on a few hours of sleep, but I have been racing through plans. *This birthday for Zach. Soon he and Toban will be moving back to Canada alone. Someone is going to need to buy him ski pants. Wouldn't it be fun to get Toban something a little stupid for our last Christmas together? A motorcycle?* These final precious mo-ments.

I take a deep breath. I had been hallucinating there for a moment, imagining that I could live in ordinary time with everyone else. I must accept what is, which is . . . Alberta. The air is crisp and cold. I shake my head a little, trying to focus on the man in front of me.

Joe's shaggy ponytail is gone, but, good, he's still

morally committed to the leather jackets and black T-shirts he wore in high school when he was in a band called Serrated Scalpel. He looks older, more professorial, but, oh great, he kept his piercings.

He looks at me and wrinkles his nose. "What?"

"I didn't mean to be gone so long."

He smiles. "And I didn't mean to live here."

We look around. Mennonites are wonderful at these thoughtful silences.

"All my time is yours," he says finally. "Kim and the kids are back at the house and we'll get dinner together later."

"This might be my last trip ever, so . . . do you want to do everything?"

"One hundred percent."

"Do you have any statues of the world's largest things nearby?"

He digs out his phone and checks the map. The world's largest Ukrainian sausage is two hours in the opposite direction.

"It promises to be the tallest piece of meat on the earth," he says solemnly.

For the next three days, we stay up late, walking the length of the town again and again and drinking Slur-

pees with vodka in the parking lot behind the 7-Eleven.
We stop to contemplate church architecture and debate the religious history of settlements in western
Canada. We worry about heaven, complain about
mutual friends who never deserved us, and skin an elk
for reasons I can't entirely re-create. I give a lecture I
don't remember to a crowd that claps at the end. By
the time I head to the airport, Joe's family has planned
the decorations for Zach's birthday party, which they
thoughtfully tuck into my luggage.

"I don't know how to give this goodbye," I say,
crushed into a group hug at the departure gate.

"Then we won't. We will simply say . . . there is the
world's largest Easter egg not far from here," says Joe,
and we have to start the hugs again from the beginning.

I SING THE ENTIRETY of "Happy Birthday" as
loudly as I want, lingering on the high notes and hovering over his sleeping form. There is nothing more
beautiful to me than the good-natured way that Zach
smiles even as he is pulled unwillingly into a new day,
rubbing his bleary eyes.

"Welcome to the best day of my life," I crow. "This

is the day that an extremely bossy baby pushed his way into the world and moved into my house."

"I'm not bossy," he yawns. "I'm Zach."

"And you are four years old today." I am kissing his ears and his forehead and his cheeks, which he barely tolerates.

"I'm not four," he insists. "That hasn't happened yet."

I was as surprised as anyone to learn that Zach was only going to turn four at the precise moment that he blew out the candles on his cake. He loudly declared this to his assembled guests—a unicorn, princess, lobster, and four superheroes. What followed was a great deal of singing and crying as the unicorn was dragged off the dining table for clawing her way toward the cake but the adults admirably carried the tune. None of the clamor bothered the burgundy dragon, with his bright yellow wings, who surveyed his kingdom with relish. Zach made his silent wish and blew out all four candles in a half-dozen tries, mostly because he got distracted and sprinted around the lawn roaring at squirrels. By the time I pulled the costume off his clammy body and into some pajamas for bed, he had forgotten what he wished for altogether.

I hear a knock at the side door as I am pulling down

the streamers and clearing away the paper plates. It's my doctor friend, Max, here to talk about the new scan results.

"Well, Zach got older. That's two more years than I expected." I shrug, tears pooling in my eyes.

Max looks around for a moment as if not sure whether to hug me or start cleaning, and settles for wiping off the table to set down his leather briefcase and pull out his laptop.

"This is . . ." He shakes his head. "It's terrible. I'm sorry. Let's try to figure out what happened, okay? We'll dig until we know as much as we can."

I open a drawer and, with both hands, pull out hundreds of pages of medical reports, which I plop down between us.

"As you are well aware," I begin, "there is a new tumor that managed to break through the immuno-therapy drugs at an alarming speed. That is very bad news. So I went through all of my past scans and highlighted anything that the radiologists singled out for suspicion. I figured that's a good start." I push a few hundred pages over the table at him. There are scribbles and yellow highlighter markings everywhere.

Max pulls out his glasses and begins to thumb through the pages. It is slow work, but we develop our own rhythm, me reading the medical reports aloud as he flicks through my CT and MRI images. ("I'm not a radiologist," he apologizes, "so you'll have to take all this with a grain of salt.") As we sift through the data, he pauses to explain and interpret different categories of alarm. Lungs are fickle, so spots might appear and disappear on a whim. These flecks of dark matter across my liver were once malignant, he guesses, but they should be dead tissue by now if the immunotherapy worked. What did they decide about your peritoneal cavity? How many lymph nodes tested positive for cancer? We comb out bits of data like lice.

"Wait," he says, rubbing his forehead. "Read that last bit again."

"It says that in segment four there was a two-centimeter area of dark matter. That's the tumor here in . . . Wait, then it says there was 'signal dropout.'"

We both frown.

"Have you ever heard that term before?" I ask.

"Never . . ." he replies. My fingers are flying across my computer keys now as I research the term, its origins in radiology, something about how the frequencies can be glitchy . . .

"Check the bottom," he says suddenly. "Did a second radiologist sign off on it?"

"No."

He grabs the report from my hands and races through it, stops, and then whips out his phone to dial.

"Hi! Sorry it's late. Thanks for taking my call."

I am too nervous to sit, so I start cleaning the kitchen with an ear to the conversation, though they lose me from the get-go. But it is only a few minutes before Max puts the phone on the counter and slaps it for good measure.

"Signal dropout!" he whoops. "Signal dropout! There was signal dropout in segment four. My favorite radiologist, bless him for taking my call, said that it's common to have a poor signal in that area of the scan."

He starts typing away, and soon he has my radiology report in front of him on the screen.

"Well . . . that would do it," he says quietly. "The report has been amended. My guess is that a second radiologist had the chance to look at it, and now it doesn't say tumor here at all."

"What does it say?" I am breathless.

"It says . . . 'fat deposit.'"

We burst out laughing, high on discovery.

"So you're saying I'm not dying. I'm just . . . fat?"

"A two-centimeter fat deposit is—"

"Is not cancer!" I yell.

"It is decidedly *not* cancer."

"I'd prefer my liver nice and plump anyway," I say definitely, patting my stomach, thanking Max profusely before he makes a quick exit so I can tell everyone the news.

When I write to Dr. Cartwright late into the night, I tell him gently what has happened. How I was "surprised," how Max helped me do this digging, that our "impression" is that I do not have a new tumor but could this be confirmed by the radiology team? Dr. Cartwright responds immediately with an anemic acknowledgment that, yes, the spot is not a tumor but that he wishes I would come to him first when I "feel this way." When we meet face-to-face, he will seem very surprised that I believed I had cancer after I was, you know, told I had cancer and had been instructed to begin radiation. He is a lawyer's dream. Admit nothing but her anxiety.

Too exhausted for sleep, I creep quietly into the dragon's lair. Zach is barely visible, buried under the weight of an enormous toy crane he had been given hours before, his hand curled around the boom. I tug it from his grasp and, as he sighs, I climb into bed beside him. The way he buries his head into my neck, the way my chin rests on his sticky forehead, how he still smells like grass and buttercream icing. I am not buried in the prairies or under piles of paperwork. I am here.

——

CHAPTER EIGHT

Befores & Afters

"SO WHAT DOES THIS MEAN, AGAIN?" I ASK
Dr. Cartwright.

He is staring at my chart, looking incredibly
pleased. I am back to where I was before: stable. Not
moving forward, not moving backward. He reminds
me again that, by all measures, I should have died
long ago, but now it is likely that most (if not all) of
the cancer cells are dead. But here I am sitting with
Toban, my brows furrowed and fingers on my temples
like I'm staving off a migraine.

He begins to tell me something vague about how
we can't know, this is the edge of what science can tell

us; but this is familiar ground. I have built a home here on the side of this cliff. With each scan, I can feel the upward draft from the deep. And I can stand it for however long it takes for a lab tech, two radiologists, then an oncologist, to get back to me and remind me that we get to do this again in a few months.

"But what does it mean?" I ask again. "You're not saying I'm cured. But I've met the definition of survival. Can I . . . move on?"

My mind is reeling now. A good friend is pregnant with her third child ("Just in under the wire," she said with a laugh), and my neighbor is filing paperwork to be a legal guardian for their fourth foster child. I have been determined to celebrate their abundance, heaping Zach's love-worn belongings into their hands and pushing them out the door like Thanksgiving leftovers. *Take the stroller. Wait, I think there are matching pants for that sweater.*

But there's that hitch in my voice when I talk to strangers—"No, he's an only child"—and the way I industriously transformed the second bedroom into an office and scrubbed my closet of my last pregnancy. I was burning the ships behind me. *We will not return.*

Except . . . maybe.

"I could have that baby," I blurt out. I look over at Toban, who only blinks back at me.

We could restart our lives. We could be the family we imagined. We could gamble on a little more hope. I beam at them.

"Well," Dr. Cartwright says with a tight smile. "That would be a publishable event."

BY THE TIME I leave the cancer clinic, I have been set straight.

When I signed the consent form to receive immuno-therapy, I signed away my fertility for as long as I was receiving the treatment. My life hangs on the efficacy of drugs for an indeterminate period of time. And what effect do these drugs have on a woman's fertility? What about a growing fetus? A pregnant woman is a host. What if my immune system goes to war against any pregnancy I am hosting? What if the drugs stop working?

There are too many questions.

Toban is silent throughout. He shakes his head as we leave. He looks exhausted.

"I don't know, Kate."

"No, it's fine. It was stupid. I just . . . I thought for a minute there that we could go back."

AMERICANS LOVE TO SAY that they have "no regrets." From the trivial to the traumatic, it seems impossible to acknowledge that sometimes you wish you could just go back. The affair? No regrets. Giving up that career? Never let that bother me. Celebrities who are interviewed after an explosive scandal squirm their way through questions until they can deliver the final line: "But it made me who I am today." We are the sum of our experiences, the story goes, and require no retrospection. The road behind us could never have led anywhere but here.

When I study the self-help industry, cataloging its thousands of bestsellers, I can't help but feel intoxicated by these grand narratives of progress. Nothing is impossible if you believe! The faces on book jackets, smiling behind titles like *The School of Greatness* or *Unleash the Power Within* are there to remind you that you can always fix your life. Eat this, and you won't get sick. Lose weight, and you'll never be lonely. Pain is inevitable, but suffering is optional.

We are a culture racing toward better tomorrows,

but suffering is the slow work of attrition. First it costs you casual friends and small talk, then retirement plans and the thrill of being cajoled into new projects.

"I have another scan this week," I say lightly, hoping to reassure my loved ones that it is safe to rejoin my orbit. There is always another scan, because this is my reality. But the people I know are often busy contending with mildly painful ambition and the possibility of reward. I try to begrudge them nothing, except I'm not alongside them anymore.

In the meantime I have been hunkered down with old medical supplies and swelling resentment. I tried— hadn't I tried?—to avoid fights and remember birthdays. I showed up for dance recitals and listened to weight-loss dreams and kept the granularity of my medical treatments in soft focus. A person like that would be easier to love, I reasoned.

I try a small experiment and stop calling my regular rotation of friends and family, hoping that they will call me back on their own. *This is not a test. This is not a test.* The phone goes quiet, except for a handful of calls. I feel heavy with a strange new grief. Is it bitter or unkind to want everyone to remember what I can't forget? Who wants to be confronted with the reality that we are all a breath away from a problem that could alter our lives completely? A friend with a very sick child said it best: I'm everyone's inspiration and no one's friend.

I am asked all the time to say that, given what I've gained in perspective, I would never go back. Who would want to know the truth? Before was better.

I CALL MY FRIEND Steve, a widower, about this second wave of loneliness.

"I've been depressed before. This isn't depression," I say.

Three years after his wife's death, Steve has been feeling similarly. We have spent hours on the phone trying to sift through the things we've lost, the things that remain. Gone is our innocence about the cost of love (astronomical) and our confidence in the future (dubious). There is considerable discussion about not wanting pain to make us narcissistic and allowing friends the latitude to describe accidentally bleaching a shirt as a "tragedy." And we fully agree that we stumbled into the heart of a mystery—that there were moments of suffering that felt unmistakably like gifts.

"There was something incredibly meaningful about

the world of cancer, about embracing the full spectrum of reality," I tell him over the phone one night. "Even though I was dying, I have never felt more alive."

"I know what you mean," he agrees quickly. "When my wife died, I felt such a surge of determination to always know what really matters and to really live out each day."

We fall into a steep silence, thinking of all the people, now gone, who we had promised to honor by living fully.

There is a pang of guilt as I strain to remember those early days when, suspended painfully in the present, I had been able to use my fears to see more clearly. I knew what to love. I knew who to love. I found moments of enoughness without the promise of more.

"It's draining out of me," he says finally. "That feeling of purpose."

"Me too. I thought it had changed me completely."

"Do you think we might be getting stuck here? We can't go back, but we can't move forward?" he wonders.

We have both seen this happen with other widows, other cancer patients. A beloved dies. The illness has taken too much. Or perhaps an addiction, divorce, illness, or accident strikes, and now any future has been razed and the ground has been salted so that nothing new can grow.

"I actually saw a bird do this recently."

Steve laughs. "What?"

"Last week at a gas station, I heard the weirdest sound. It took me a minute to realize that I was hearing a bird—a parrot actually—singing 'Happy Birthday' in a cage behind the counter. So I asked. Oliver the Cockatoo used to belong to a very successful real estate agent who died, and Oliver bit every new owner and flapped his wings in their faces. So I walked over and Oliver and I sang a few rounds of 'Happy Birthday' together in the most depressing way."

Steve laughs even louder.

"But the man behind the counter said, 'Lady, I wouldn't bother. That bird is only forty years old, and he's going to live another forty. But Oliver is a one-man bird.'"

"*A one-man bird!*" cries Steve.

"So yeah! I think you can stop living at any time."

"Well, shit," he says finally, trying to regain his composure. "I guess life is going to need more courage than I thought."

—

I AM BACK IN my psychologist's office. Peter specializes in behavioral therapy, which is wonderful because I'm not sure how to behave anymore.

"I don't know how to move forward without knowing what will happen next," I say, shifting in my seat.

I've been searching for an oncologist who might help me understand what the research says about my survival. How are the other patients in the clinical trial and on this immunotherapy drug faring? Did any of them have their ports removed? Did they have children? Can anyone move on?

"What kind of language do the doctors use to describe your prognosis now?" asks the psychologist.

"My oncologist called it a 'durable remission' the other day. He won't answer any of my questions about other patients. So I found the names of other leading doctors and picked the most famous one with the largest cohort of patients. Then I put down a lot of money, and I flew to New York to see him."

My psychologist leans forward. "And what did the famous doctor say?"

"It was awful. I argued with everyone. I asked the junior doctor if most patients responded to the immunotherapy. I asked how many continued to re-spond. I asked about genetic variables. She gave me the runaround, and we argued until she admitted that she *could* tell me that information, but she didn't know what the information would 'mean to me.'"

The psychologist and I gape at each other.

"I bet you had something to say to that," he said in a low voice.

I remember what happened next in slow motion. The famous doctor finally entered the examination room, sat down, and the same argument played out again. I volleyed the first questions lightly, suggesting enough familiarity with their colleagues, their re-search, and their world to speed things up, building to the big question: *Based on your clinical experience, what does your intuition say about the long-term sur-vival of patients like me?*

He wouldn't answer. I tried again. *Please, I have tried to understand, but I am at the limits of what I can know as a regular person. And it will be years before your clinical trial results will be made public. You are learning things along the way and I just want to make use of what you are learning!*

He wouldn't bite. We had a long discussion about

whether I was taking my multivitamin. I tried one last time. *Look, I put in all the money, all the time, all the research to get here. After four years of being told that we can't know, the truth is that some people do know. You know.*

The famous doctor looked at me evaluatively.

"Why is this so important to you?" he asked.

"Why?! *Because I want to live!*"

He let out a long sigh.

" 'Live,' " he repeated. The word was suspended in the air for a moment. "But what is mortality anyway?"

I felt the blood rush to my face.

"It's dying before your kid goes to kindergarten," I spat back. "I'm glad you're in a position to be philosophical about this."

We stared at each other for a long moment, before he softened his expression and smiled again. "Well," he said, "let's take another look at your charts . . ." In the end, he suggested that I get another genetic screening and return in six months.

Telling the psychologist all of this, I suddenly feel exhausted. I pull my feet up onto the armchair and hug my knees, taking a moment to compose myself. My psychologist clears his throat gently.

"Kate, that is a betrayal. You had every reason to believe that you were going to be cared for, and then you weren't."

I try to say thank you, but there are only wet sniffling sounds.

"You have been left in this heightened present forever," he says finally.

"Yes . . . exactly. What would you prescribe if I were afraid of something less existential. Like tall buildings?" I wonder.

"Well, we might take you up onto a roof and sit there until you relaxed. It's called exposure therapy."

"What if you took me up on the roof, and it caved in? *Multiple times*," I say loudly.

"It would take a lot longer," he says with a laugh.

"Fear has helped keep me alive. I learned to read medical reports, doctors' expressions, clinical trial notifications . . ."

"Fear has been a wonderful friend to you," he agrees. "But you can't stay in this state of extreme vigilance. You can't . . . live here anymore." How gently he lays this at my feet. *You cannot stay.*

"Is there a reasonable time for me to stop being afraid? Medicine refuses to give me an answer to that."

"Do you need to stop being afraid to move forward? What do you have to lose?" he pushes back.

"Everything!" I exclaim, immediately teary. "I could lose Zach! I could lose Toban! I could lose all my plans and trips and stupid dreams!"

"Right!" he says.

"So you want me to have courage or something approximating it?"

We are laughing hard now.

"So it would seem," he replies, trying to settle down.

Now that I have every good reason to be afraid; now that I know what it feels like when the earth buckles; now that I'm afraid to stay as I am, but more afraid to move forward: What if I forget what I learned? And what if I can't learn to hope again?

I look over at Peter and smile nervously.

"Well . . . there is something on the horizon. I've been thinking about what I never thought would happen. I'd like to turn forty. Maybe I could let myself look forward to that without hedging my bets quite so much?"

"That's an excellent idea."

—

"Name."

"Catherine Bowler."

"Date of birth."

"Six, sixteen, 1980."

"Can you tell me what procedure you'll be having today?"

I gesture to the device buried in my pectoral muscle, the outline of a triangle visibly straining against my skin. I needed the port while I was getting regular infusions of chemotherapy and immunotherapy, but now that I am on a regular schedule of wait-and-see scans I'm not certain that I still do. I might, but I have decided to be painfully optimistic.

"I am having my port removed."

The surgical nurse looks like he was poured from concrete, and I marvel that his enormous hand doesn't snap the plastic pen as he scribbles on my chart. He barely looks up.

"Or we could do it right here," I continue, eyeing him. "You could reach inside my chest cavity and rip the port from my beating heart with your bare hands?"

He laughs so loudly and for so long that I start to have a different kind of day. His name is Patrick and he hails from the island province of Newfoundland, Canada, and would I like to meet all the other Canadian nurses? Of course. Yes, I can bring Toban back until the last moment before my surgery and keep my own slippers. By the time the anesthesiologist arrives, the Canadian nurses have enumerated every good reason to injure another man in an adult hockey league (boasting, dawdling, and the unpardonable sin of "dipsy-doodling"), and I have named the surgeon who asked me out on a date after inserting this very port. They howl before we all eventually conclude his invitation was both illegal and a wonderful vote of confidence in my survival.

"The hospital places a strong emphasis on follow-up care," says Patrick.

This tide of goodwill takes me to the moment when the drugs have been administered and the procedure begins. *Wait, where are you from again? I've never been to Newfoundland, but my sister used to live in Nova Scotia. Wasn't Newfoundland a British colony until 1949? I meant to ask you, where are you from again?* I can hear my own voice, strong and clear, and a deep rumbling in response; but I am swimming in a cold, deep lake. I kick my legs to dive deeper still. Down, down, down. I can feel the weight of the water beginning to squeeze the air from my lungs. Suddenly I can't breathe. There is thrumming in my eardrums and then a hard yank as I feel something being torn from my chest.

"Show it to me," I call out to no one. *"Show it to me!"*

Then all at once, nothingness. Not darkness. Just nothing at all.

Hours later, I am grateful for the quiet moment when Patrick volunteers to help Toban wheel me to the entrance of the hospital.

"I haven't seen that in a while," he says quietly. "You should have been completely out with the drugs we were giving you. But you fought *hard*."

I am struggling against a surge of embarrassment.

"I wasn't exactly advised to do this," I admit. "I've been making all my own big medical decisions for a while now, and this one felt . . . tricky. I'm moving forward even though I have no idea what's . . . going to happen."

He smiles a little too knowingly.

"Wait, did I ask you to show me my own port? In the middle of the surgery? I did. I really did." I close my eyes, hoping to evaporate into thin air.

He laughs again. "You were real sure about it. You wanted to see it, then you wanted to keep it."

I glance down at the thick gauze taped to my chest wall. I am alone in my body again.

We are at the entryway now.

"That's it. You're on your own now." He looks down at me in the wheelchair and pats me on the head with his giant paw. "You'd be great in the rink," he says, shaking his head, and I am starting to believe him.

"MOM . . ." ZACH TRAILS OFF.

We are at the edge of saying good night. There are still Band-Aids sticking out here and there, and I am moving slowly these days, but bedtimes proceed at the perfect pace. They are sticky sweet and always full of a great deal of sudden wondering when I am about to leave his room and turn out the light. *Do pirates hate land? Is cheese funny? Do you know what an isthmus is?*

"Mom . . ." he starts again. "Mom, do you think anyone has love like us? We have gorilla hearts that beat: love-love, love-love, love-love." He thumps his chest with his small fist.

"Gorilla hearts!" I exclaim, slowly easing myself

down again to his height. "What a perfect descrip-tion. Yes, we have big, dumb gorilla hearts, don't we?"

My mind flits back three years to an outing with my sister Amy, who was trying to take my mind off the hospital with a trip to the zoo. But by the time we pulled into the zoo parking lot, the skies had turned to sheets of rain. We'd been stuck in a muggy car for an hour, listening to the radio over the rhythmic click of my chemotherapy pack, when I heard the sounds of muffled crying over the thrum of the rain.

"Amy," I said quietly, putting my hand on her back. She is turned away from me, her head in her hands.

"Are you okay?"

She said something, insistent but unintelligible.

"Did you say something about gorillas?"

"Yes," she cleared her throat. "I wanted to show you the gorillas."

"Sure," I said, not wanting to press. Amy has an encyclopedic knowledge of animals: animal habits, animal sounds, and animal postures, proclivities, and tricks that she paints every day into watercolors. She recently painted me a series of ostriches pausing to say, "Hey! I love you!"

She put her head back against the headrest and closed her eyes.

"Charles and Samantha are western lowland gorillas who were mated for life. But then Samantha had a stroke. While she was trying to get better Charles would stay beside her every day, but then one day Samantha had another stroke and *died*. And Charles thought she was asleep and he touched her face and tried to wake her up . . ." Her eyes searched my face for understanding. "But Samantha was gone. And the keepers took her body away, but Charles . . ."

I was failing to suppress a surge of hysterical giggles.

"Amy!" I said loudly, trying unsuccessfully to sound equally emotional as I put my arms around her.

"Charles still sits all day every day in the place where he last saw her!" she wailed.

"Oh, honey."

"He is still waiting for her now!"

The parking lot was a shallow lake, and the car an island.

"Sweetie, but do you think that maybe we aren't only talking about gorillas?"

"We are only talking about gorillas!" she cried, as I tucked a strand of her dark hair behind her ear.

"Okay!" I said, attempting a combination of seriousness and enthusiasm. "Then let's go talk about gorillas."

We clambered out of the car and bolted across the parking lot and into the zoo where, other than the occasional groundskeeper, there was not a person in sight. We exchanged a look of pure delight, and took off. We sprinted from shelter to shelter, shrieking through the downpour, on the lookout for drenched animals as we raced by. The bison shuffled around looking like wet rugs, while the flint-gray rhinoceroses were slick and immobile. The cheetahs had cleverly tucked themselves under the branches of tall trees and the giraffes—always the showstopper—paced back and forth under a leafy canopy. A camel stood dolefully in the center of a field as if waiting for further instruction.

Only in the gorilla enclosure did we quiet for a moment to see Charles sitting in the dirt, his massive black frame elegant and still. And we stopped to give our respects, more than a little awed by the way hearts go on beating, never sorry to be broken.

—

CHAPTER NINE

Flesh & Blood

"MAYBE I SHOULD TRAIN FOR A RACE."

My mother stops mixing the pancake batter she solemnly promised my son will be less fluffy than it was the day before. These are the wonderful tragedies we have been having this summer, a son who picks the chocolate chips out of his pancakes to examine each carefully like a tiny Gordon Ramsay.

"You might be thinking, did my daughter ever run? But I did. I did sometimes," I continue, popping a handful of chewable vitamins into my mouth.

She studies me for a moment. "I think your body has been through a lot," she says, too carefully, returning her gaze to the skillet.

Indifference is one of the great performances attempted between parents and children, but it is an art form my mother has never perfected. She is the parent who fought back tears when her daughters wanted to get their belly buttons pierced (thank you, Britney Spears) or drive on a country road after dark.

"What are you doing today?" she would ask my teenage self.

"I'd like to say 'prostitution,' but kids call it 'sex work' nowadays, okay bye!" I would yell, slamming the door behind me.

"She's a *bit much,*" I would tell my friends, rolling my eyes as we pulled away from the house. The first time I sucked in my stomach or turned sideways in the mirror to see myself as I was seen, watched, appraised, I forgot—all at once—that I had always been that woman's child. A body made whole by the miracle of conception and gestation and birth. Apparently adolescence is the process of believing that you belong not to someone but to everyone.

My mother, no matter how grateful she is to good medicine, will always see my surgeons as butchers. They cut thick lines that crisscrossed under my clavicle, bisected my stomach, and swooped down from my sternum. And when she saw me lying on her couch, my shirt accidentally exposing the puckered seams of my scars, she couldn't help herself. "If you don't mind," she said quickly, and leaned over and kissed my stomach before I could reply. This is the burden of a mother's love, how it must hover without landing.

I hear it when I introduce my own child saying, "Oh, him? I made him with my body. It's no big deal, but it took the better part of a year." And they laugh, and I get a moment to pretend it is not precisely what I think when I gaze at him sleeping, his shirt pulled up over his soft tummy. *Oh, that. Flesh of my flesh.*

I should be feeling better these days, but there is an intense nothingness that I experience when I see myself in the mirror. Not self-loathing, not frustration, but simply nothing at all. It may have started when, in the early days of my treatment, the physician's assistant casually told me that the sooner I got used to the idea of dying, the better. But I certainly understood it shortly after that when I kept a dental appointment for a routine checkup. My dentist was young and pretty and fresh out of dental college, and when she reviewed my new medical history on her clipboard, she paused and took off her mask.

"I don't understand," she said in her sweet, high voice. "Why are you even here?"

I thought I was something, but I might be nothing at all.

"I'm not special," I stammer as I try to explain this to my friends. "No, I mean, I am special to the people who love me. Thank you. I just don't believe I'm . . . terribly valuable. Does that make sense?" I make people feel uncomfortable by saying it, so I stop.

I have walked this hard thought to the end of the line: I am probably replaceable. When I needed to make plans for a world without me—my son's new mother, my husband's less difficult wife—it became easier and easier to imagine.

Everyone else seems real enough. I watch my colleagues go to work and talk about the news and then argue about footnotes in a way that seems entirely reasonable to me. But a weed has been growing where a feeling of natural worth once bloomed. And I can't root it out.

I try different forms of meditation, breathing exercises, routines, and affirmations. Nothing. I lose weight, I gain weight. Nothing. I hire a body-image specialist and fill out workbooks about healthy eating and confidence and loving myself.

Somewhere between the hospital and my Instagram

feed a feeling slipped away. *This body is my home.* No matter how hard I try, that's gone.

"Do you think my face is melting off?" I ask Chelsea solemnly.

We have been openly fretting about the possibility of "losing our luster."

"You have plenty of luster," Chelsea assures me, her eyes wide like she is entering a hostage negotiation. It's a horrifying phrase we coined to describe the consequences of aging, neglect, and something more. We had noticed that sometimes people can simply fade. For reasons that seem mysterious, some people no longer sparkle. And looking at them now, I wonder if that person is me.

The polish of youth has been wearing off and I'm confused about whether to hide the evidence. A whole new wave of advertising has been reserved for me, the newly christened "middle-aged woman," to explain what I should be worried about. Crinkles around the eyes and softness around the belt have been relabeled as "crow's feet" and "muffin tops." Those thin white lines—what remains of a successful C-section and a baby's triumphal entry—will require a tummy tuck with a six-week recovery, but the "bat wings" on my arms can be fixed with a studio membership, where other anxious novices will take up a stationary bicycle or a spot at the barre. We are learning our box-dye numbering systems to eliminate "stubborn grays," but truly nothing seems as harrowing as the hair surgeries for men with dreams of middle management.

Should we hate the evidence that we have survived?

I think about a friend who finished a heavy bout of radiation therapy for her breast cancer and showed me, with horror, what was left of her thick brown bangs.

"Look at these sad little tufts!" she says, tugging at wisps of hair against her forehead. "They are hideous."

But they were not hideous, and her hair would have been entirely unremarkable to anyone who did not know that it had once been a tad thicker. There are countless people I love who are radically altered by their course of treatment, losing more than hair and eyelashes, some marked by ragged scars or amputated limbs. Ours are small, personal losses.

"Are we mourning our youth?" I ask Chelsea finally. "I'm constantly confused because aging isn't the enemy. I am really *hoping* to age."

There is a vast wing of the wellness industry whose purpose it is to stop time. The suburbs are awash with Botox parties, CrossFit memberships, anti-aging drugstore creams, and rumors about Karen's face lift. The upper classes have their spa culture, recreational plastic surgeries, "wintering" and "summering," and recent acquaintanceship with a Silicon Valley tech entrepreneur hoping for future reanimation through cryogenic freezing. There are bona fide miracles hiding in the nutrients of every ordinary and exotic food ("Try the mushrooms in Bali.") and proven principles to decelerate cellular aging ("Erase the years—in only thirty minutes a day!"). Turn on the television day or night to see celebrity experts give "breakthrough" advice about fat-blasting exercises, "revolutionary" routines, and "shocking" results. There is no aspect of mortality—from infertility to cancer to death itself—left untouched by the tireless merchants of limitless health.

But as much as I roll my eyes at their outrageous promises, I miss the possibility of being decorative.

After years of hard treatment, I have a body nothing like the one my mother made. But I had studied the emaciated frames in the chemotherapy infusion rooms, propped up by the strong bones of those that loved them, and sworn that I would never be so super-ficial as to complain about flesh again.

I have heard this confusion about the importance or irrelevance of appearance echoed by other patients toying with the word *survivor*. We may have stopped buying clothes or shaved our heads, given up on small luxuries or on buying something as simple as scar cream. "What's the point?" we say, shaking our heads. We left those fantasies on the operating table. Who would fault a body that has survived so much and asked for so little?

Derek the plastic surgery resident smiles with-out teeth. He has greased back his long hair and runs his hands through it, repeatedly, as he looks at me. Already a nurse has been checking to ensure I am a machine with working parts: blood pressure—low; weight—within range; temperature—average. *Are you sleeping? How much pain are you in?* I can be calibrated and recalibrated.

He asks me to remember all the surgeries I have had in order, but I lose track because I'm standing al-most naked in an open gown and suffering from an incurable case of Canadian small talk. What made him choose plastic surgery? Did he see last night's episode of *The Bachelor*? His mom must be so proud.

He crouches down in front of me, making an inventory of every one of my surgeries from a clipboard and pausing to match each with the scars he can see several inches from his eyeballs. *Is there a great reason I have to be almost naked here?* I am a human display case.

Finally, he stands up.

"I would think that someone with your history would be grateful that it's not much worse."

"When you look at my body, you think: 'Hey, this could be worse,'" I paraphrase.

Derek gives a tight smile. "Given the number of surgeries you've had, you need to consider what a fortunate position you're in."

"Derek," I begin, using his name and happily recalling that he has never invited me to do so. "Derek, we are both in our thirties. Except I've been living with Stage Four cancer. And I think you want me to tell you that I'm grateful."

"You don't have to be grateful, but you have to understand that some people are horribly maimed."

"I am not disfigured," I agree. "I am thrilled about that. If you want to look up here at my *face*, I hope you'll see that I'm thrilled."

Derek is running his finger down a long scar across my stomach, studded like braille from surgical staples.

"I helped dig them out," I say matter-of-factly.

There is a knock at the door and two other people in lab coats enter, and, to their credit, they manage the introductions and all-around handshaking with an almost naked patient quite adeptly.

"Derek here was saying that since I didn't die and am not grossly disfigured, that I should be pretty happy with all of this," I say grandly, gesturing to my torso like a beautiful car model.

The doctor in charge leans over and takes a closer look, pinching and pushing and then standing back appraisingly with a tilt of his head.

"I can do a procedure that would dramatically alter the position of this here"—he gestures—"and the appearance of that, there." He points. "It would leave you with another long scar here but, frankly, it would look significantly better."

He wags his finger at me. "But like I tell all my patients, getting this surgery is like choosing between the new car and the ski vacation. I can give you some things, but I can't give you everything."

"I'm not asking for everything, or nothing." I glance over at Derek. "I'm just trying to figure out if I would feel more at home in my body if I didn't have quite so much evidence that it almost tried to kill me."

Suddenly I remember two things: that there is a waiting room full of women looking for breast augmentation consultations and that I am lecturing plastic surgeons on the importance of appearance. I tell this to Sarah Bessey, who I call on the way out of the clinic because, since a car accident left her in chronic pain, Sarah has been the kind of friend who understands the cost of a body that tries and fails and still has to make dinner.

"I want to say that I am happy for a body that works," I say to her, embarrassed. "And I am happy. I am deeply grateful. But I'm trying to figure out how to feel more like sunshine again and less like a well-functioning sewer system."

"Right! The body is not a meat sack: it is memory and orgasms and snuggles and swimming in the summer," she says, pausing. "It's so weird that working so hard to stay alive makes you feel less human."

We contemplate that for a moment. There are many religious traditions that argue that the spirit ought to triumph over the body in all ways. In Christianity, we rejected this as a heresy called Gnosticism in the fourth century, but wouldn't it be nice?

"You know, Sarah, dying is a great time to want to be all spirit and no flesh. Sometimes the body is a weight pulling you all the way down. And it's hard to love the stone that drowns you."

THE LAST TIME I felt whole didn't make any sense. Surgeons were harvesting cancer from my useless organs, cutting tissue into ribbons, and paperwork had been drawn up for me to sign, so yes, I knew the odds. Each day was a terrible winnowing, separating wheat from chaff, but I felt a surreal completeness. I remember clearly in the hospital how I felt this strange closeness with God, how I did not feel like dry grass. I was becoming less and less, but I was not reduced to nothing.

God's love was everywhere, sticking to everything. Love was in my husband's hand on my back, steadying me, a lightness under my feet, and all over Zach's velvety ears. I flushed with embarrassment when I described this feeling to my friends, stumbling as I tried to explain its sudden appearance (*Wasn't it there before?*), that love itself was suddenly more real to me than my own thoughts. Despair was never far away, but somehow the seams of the universe had come undone, and all the splendid, ragged edges were showing.

And they brought me closer than I've ever been to the truth of this experiment—living—and how the horror and the beauty of it feels almost blinding.

Later, when I was able to walk, I went hiking through a North Carolina forest with my friend Laura to tell her the long story of how I was coming undone but I was not unmade.

"Then please don't fuck this up, Kate," she said sagely, which sent me into hysterics. She is a therapist and one of the wisest Christians I know, so she is keenly aware that a well-placed expletive is better than all the inspiration in the world. "You have felt the mighty and indescribable love of God. It is wholeness and beauty and holiness . . . but it is not Disney World."

I laughed so hard I had to stop to lean against a tree. "Unless Disney World is performing abdominal surgeries that I'm not aware of."

"When you started to face your own death, you started to have these experiences, right?"

"Yes!" I exclaimed. "Exactly. Life felt like magic."

These moments of transcendence have been scattered everywhere like breadcrumbs.

"Those experiences of magic . . . they are the truth of our lives. But we can't get confused! Life can be rich and real. But people will want you to say that these moments make your life complete. Does everything feel wrapped up, Kate?"

"No!" I said, my mind spinning. "Is it wrong that I want to raise that kid and I want to relearn French and I want to write a children's book and I really, really want to go back to Disney World?"

I had been asking to go to Disney World my entire life, having seen an American commercial about the happiest place on earth and ever since had the niggling sense that our annual summer trips to Moose Jaw, Saskatchewan, in the back seat of an unairconditioned Datsun left something to be desired. In fact, it had become a family tradition that at the mere mention of Disney World my father would yell, "Shut up girls! I'm not done not taking you yet!" This continued until I was twenty-six and I took myself after completing my doctoral dissertation exams. I immediately mailed my parents a bill with a note that read, *There. You took me. It was glorious.*

I wanted to report back that I had visited for ironic reasons, but the cold truth is that I found the entire experience so wondrous that tears streamed down my face at the sight of it.

"This is the parking lot," Toban had said, appropriately concerned.

It is a mystery to me why some mere minutes transform into moments, hovering outside of time. And how they ebb and flow, stirring wonder and the ache for more. I know the love of a God who is beyond all wanting, but the more I live, the more I want and want and want.

"There is no such thing as a finished life, Kate," Laura said, at last. "Eventually we get eternity with God. But in the meantime there's crappy regular stuff that, if we are really lucky, might feel like a trip to Central Florida."

I think back to my first year of cancer treatment when, every Wednesday in the airport, passengers were hugging and crying and running to catch the nonstop to Paris, as I waited under the escalator for a plane to take me home. In these moments, I starved. Everywhere I saw endless and beautiful possibilities.

Except one night, I was waiting to board next to the nonstop flight to Orlando, Florida. It was the aviation superhighway to Walt Disney World Resort and everywhere I looked, Mickey Mouse ears were tearing around the terminal. But it was deep into the evening and the gate was strewn with families in various states of disarray. A young mom was changing a diaper out in the open, glassy-eyed teenagers were tethered to screens, and elementary school children had gotten loopy. The Sleepover Sillies had taken hold, and parents were starting to lose their cool.

A grown man in mouse ears was standing in the corner with his wife, his arms crossed, the words between them fast and heated. Their two boys were being brothers, expertly pissing each other off, pushing and hooting with laughter. But they were not prepared for the moment of detonation when their dad wheeled around, pulled off his mouse ears, and threw them to the floor.

"This is a once-in-a-lifetime experience!" he shouted, flushed with anger. "And we are going to *make some family memories dammit*!"

And I laughed until my stomach hurt and my eyes watered. Who could want anything more?

———

WITH MY FORTIETH BIRTHDAY around the corner, I am ready. I have resurrected the old bucket list and have concluded that this will be the season of making other people's dreams come true (with a few detours to check off some of mine). I plan a trip to take my son to Holland with his grandparents so he can see where his grandmother was born. I sketch a plan to see the World's Largest Ball of String in Valley View, Texas. I reserve a pub to host a high school reunion, and I have rallied a team to participate in a five-kilometer race to benefit colon cancer research, complete with T-shirts that read WE'VE GOT THE RUNS.

A few days before my birthday, I am sitting in my yard, when I receive a text from one of my Kates from No Kate Left Behind. It's a press release announcing the results of the clinical trial led by the famous doctor I visited, Dr. What Is Mortality Anyway. Most of the doctors I'd contacted, including mine, were waiting nervously for this larger clinical trial to release its findings on the outcomes of its participants. I read the first page.

Most of us were dead.

—

CHAPTER TEN

Unfinished Cathedrals

THE TRUTH IS THERE ON THE PAGE. SOME OF US responded to the immunotherapy drug and lived; and many did not respond and died. Others died because they were placed in a control group and denied immunotherapy until their cancer spread out of control. I feel like I am free-falling. Hadn't Dr. Cartwright joked about this? The lab rat. Is that what we are?

I close myself in my office, take out my laptop, and begin hammering away, tears dripping down my face. After years of asking for facts that seemed locked away, I feel like I have finally been handed a key. Digging into the details of this trial leads me to a government database, and soon, hours and days of researching fly by. I had always felt intimidated by science, but I can see now that my training as a historian is enough to build the architecture of an argument, what happened to them, what has been happening to me.

There are approximately one hundred trials being run around the world for patients like me, recruited because our genetic profiles make us more likely to respond to immunotherapy. Scientists are focused on cracking the code of what cures us in the hope that they might apply that knowledge to cure the greater population. This is the modern Space Race—the cure for every cancer—which will save millions of lives each year and earn billions in revenue. These immunotherapy drugs must be tested on people before they can receive government approval to be sold, but the cost is astronomical. So hospitals that cannot afford it may accept "partnerships" with multi-billion-dollar pharmaceutical corporations.

I call experts in clinical trial research, psychology, and ethics, and they explain: clinical trials do not provide traditional medical care. A typical cancer patient will have an oncology, radiology, and surgical team at their disposal to discern a treatment plan designed for their direct benefit. *How are you feeling? Let's look at the scan and see where we should go from here.* A clinical trial participant will have few choices to make and may even be subjected to further risk for the benefit of the study. While I always knew that my medical treatment could be harsh, painful, and potentially deadly, I never realized that I was not a patient and did not have a doctor. I was a "study participant" assigned to a scientist.

All along, I wanted a formula for how to live, and cancer treatment had provided the clearest one of all. *Follow the rules. Keep to the schedule. Trust the experts. Smile! You're so lucky.* So I was grateful when I was enrolled. Grateful when I could barely walk anymore. Grateful when my hair stopped growing and a paper cut would bleed for days. Well done, good and faithful patient. You were grateful.

I am staring at this mountain of data I've collected, the slope of each graph, the sums that are neatly arranged into rows and columns quantifying each human life. And I can find no place to add the numbers that would express the immensity of what has been lost. My hopes were simple—I wanted to survive for my son. How many of those people needed a bit more time with their grandchildren or would have enjoyed another trip with a friend. How many began to believe that maybe they were disposable after all. I can see that there is no accounting for the things we've done, or for the things done to us.

I TURNED FORTY JUST as the unimaginable happened to everyone, all at once. The whole world was overcome by a deadly disease, and we all had to take shelter, the lives we'd imagined suspended in midair. When I finished sifting through all the clinical trial data in the middle of it, I had nothing to do but survive the feeling that some pain is for no reason at all. It became clearer than ever that life is not a series of choices. So often the experiences that define us are the ones we didn't pick. Cancer. Betrayal. Miscarriage. Job loss. Mental illness. A novel coronavirus.

All the flights to Holland have been canceled. The high school reunion will have to be rescheduled for another year, when we can laugh in each other's faces and pass tacos down the table. Month after month crawls by. In almost every measurable way, my family is faring worse since the advent of COVID-19. We are trapped in a country apart from our entire extended family in Canada, including my younger sister, who gives birth to a baby girl I cannot hold. I have a delicate immune system, so I can't enter a grocery store or risk an outdoor patio with friends. These realities would almost be manageable if they could be taken one by one. It is irrepressibly familiar, the sense that the world is suddenly growing smaller and the time growing shorter. I am heavy with the thought of each person I know who needed these months to wander or rest, find their match or start all over, who need the chance to say every hello and goodbye to each delicious moment, unrestricted. Instead, I hear updates about freezing eggs and living without touch, homeschooling without respite and worrisome symptoms without checkups. A wake takes place without fanfare over Zoom, and a wedding is on hold indefinitely. I recognize their unspoken fear: Are we wasting precious days?

At first, the American middle class seemed to experience a surge of collective resolve. There were silver linings everywhere. All the time saved by eliminating the commute would surely translate into more family dinners and long-delayed date nights. Sourdough starters and suburban chicken coops and vegetable gardens popped up all over social media to showcase the shocking benefits of modern homesteading.

Carpe diem! You got a Peloton! Make a bucket list that includes the beach body you'll sculpt from the free weights in the garage. Count your blessings. Be more present. Hadn't you always wanted to spend more time with your family?

It's very alluring, this bit of agency in the midst of an immobilizing plague. But no matter how carefully we schedule our days, master our emotions, and try to wring our best life now from our better selves, we cannot solve the problem of finitude. We will always want more. We need more. We are carrying the weight of caregiving and addiction, chronic pain and uncertain diagnosis, struggling teenagers and kids with learning disabilities, mental illness and abusive relationships. A grandmother has been sheltering without a visitor for months, and a friend's business closed its doors. Doctors, nurses, and frontline workers are acting as levees, feeling each surge of the disease crash against them. My former students, now serving as pastors and chaplains, are in hospitals giving last rites in hazmat suits. They volunteer to be the last person to hold his hand. To smooth her hair.

The truth of the pandemic is the truth of all suffering: that it is unjustly distributed. Who bears the brunt? The homeless and the prisoners. The elderly and the children. The sick and the uninsured. Immigrants and people needing social services. People of color and LGBTQ people. The burdens of ordinary evils—discrimination, brutality, predatory lending, illegal evictions, and medical exploitation—roll back on the vulnerable like a heavy stone. All of us struggle against the constraints placed on our bodies, our commitments, our ambitions, and our resources, even as we're saddled with inflated expectations of invincibility. This is the strange cruelty of suffering in America, its insistence that everything is still possible.

God, let me see things clearly. I must accept the world as it is, or break against the truth of it: my life is made of paper walls. And so is everyone else's.

A FEW YEARS AGO, in between scans, I decided to make the pilgrimage with my family to see one of the seven natural wonders of the world, the Grand Canyon. A worthy bucket-list item. Just off Route 66, I found a tiny chapel surrounded by ponderosa pine. No towns for miles. Curious, I tried the door and, finding it unlocked, tentatively walked inside.

The room was a miniature sanctuary, unheated and inelegant. The floor was loose gravel, and someone had nailed together some benches to face a chunk of stone serving as an altar. But the light of the setting sun—an incandescent orange—poured through the windows and lit up the walls, which were covered with graffiti both fresh and faded.

I ran my fingers along the black ink covering the altar and the pen marks gouging the soft wooden walls. Almost every inch of it was covered with words.

I miss you every day.

Please let my daughter be the way she was before.

Did you make it to heaven, my love?

Helen, I am weak. But you already knew that.

I looked up. Hundreds of slips of paper were stuffed into the rafters and seams in the wall. All the people who have fallen into the cracks in the universe, undone by the smallest tragedies. We try to outsmart our limitations and our bad, bad luck, but here we are, shouting the truth into the abyss. There is no cure for being human.

Someone had built a monument to the void, and it was full to the brim.

I heard the door creak open behind me, and Toban's face peeked through.

"Hello?" he called tentatively.

"Oh, hello," I said, popping my head above a pew. I was lying on my back along one of the benches, looking up at the messages scrawled on the ceiling. Toban sat down beside me and placed a gentle hand on my head.

He tipped his head up, taking in the ceiling, neither of us speaking.

"I used to think we were the only ones."

"Me too," I agree.

We all live like this, without assurances, without formulas, desperate for the secret to carrying on.

"Do you think anyone would mind if I added a little something?" I asked quickly.

Toban raised an eyebrow and gestured to the chaotic scrawl around us.

"A moment of privacy then, sir," I answered with a

smile, tearing a strip out of my notebook and taking out a pen.

I wrote down a phrase, got up on the bench, and stuffed the slip of paper in the wall as high as I could reach.

"What did you decide?" he wondered when we climbed back into the truck.

"It was something Mr. Boothe used to say," I replied. I love thinking about him at the chalkboard, goading us into advanced math problems as he publicly suffered from the disease infecting all good teachers—too much faith in humanity.

Dum spiro spero, he would say, shaking his head.

While I breathe, I hope.

MY FATHER'S GREAT FAILURE had been sitting in a filing cabinet for forty years. It was a letter from the editors of Cambridge University Press, a single paragraph sparing no sarcasm to inform him that the manuscript of his doctoral dissertation was so grossly overdue that it was no longer welcome. The submission was supposed to be his first book, the consummation of a decade of painstaking research, and his ladder out of the purgatory of adjunct labor. But books never tell you when they are finished, and a depressive mind could never be sure it mattered anyway.

My father received the news of his failure with devastating acceptance, as if relieved to hear it confirmed. And he sealed himself in his study with the letter, where it continued to sit radioactive and unopened.

"But lately I've been thinking," mused my father on the computer screen one day. He was seated in his study surrounded by an impressive collection of historical bobbleheads and stacks of loose paper. "I saw that my unpublished dissertation is still being mentioned in scholarly books so I began poking around. And, lo and behold, there have been few developments in the history of sixteenth-century resistance theory . . ."

"Well, why don't you contact Oxford University Press? You will make a triumphant return to the guild with the fanciest book in the world! They would have to send the manuscript out to a couple other professors for their peer review but other than that . . ."

"Peers, Kate?" He spun around in his wingback chair dramatically, relishing his delivery. "Do you think I have *peers*?"

I burst out laughing. "Fine. I take your point. It's probably time to . . ."

"Yes"—he nodded—"finish at last."

I received a signed copy of the book for Christmas. He had launched his own little press to publish it himself with a lovely watercolor on the cover painted by my older sister.

"You published your dissertation at seventy years old," I called to tell him, riffling through the book with admiration. "Ah, I see here you've referred to other scholars as 'the indefatigable drones of the academic industry.'"

He chuckled. "I promise progress not perfection."

These are such small decisions, really. But aren't they all? Trying again. Getting back up. Trusting someone new. Loving extravagantly inside these numbered days.

Someday we won't need to hope. Someday we don't need courage. Time itself will be wrapped up with a bow, and God will draw us all into the eternal moment where there will be no suffering, no disease, no email.

In the meantime, we are stuck with our beautiful, terrible finitude. Our gossip and petty fights, self-hatred and refusal to check our voicemail. We get divorced, waste our time, and break our own hearts. We are cobbled together by the softest material, laughter and pets and long talks with old friends. By God's un-scrupulous love and by communities who give us a place to belong. And there is nothing particularly glamorous about us, except that we have moments when we are shockingly magnanimous before forget-ting about it the next day.

How lucky, then, that we are not failing. Our lives are not problems to be solved. We can have meaning and beauty and love, but nothing even close to resolu-tion.

Every time I imagine it, I think of my friend Rich-ard about to preach, his white liturgical robe billow-ing like laundry hanging on the line. The chill of night hung in the air as we filed into rows of folding chairs laid out on a lawn. We were there for a church service set to begin at the very break of dawn.

"Christ is risen."

A voice called and we answered without thinking. "He is risen indeed."

Richard was grinning at me, and I waved from the crowd without decorum. We had lost that some time ago, possibly during our years in a faculty-led Leon-ard Cohen cover band, but certainly when we were both diagnosed with cancer in rapid succession. He had been finishing up a sterling academic career and I had only begun, and so began our walks. Walks around the hospital. Walks around these gardens. And as we walked, we reviewed the basics: how we originally had planned on living forever; how the promise of eternal life places hope ever before us; and how relieved we were to keep our splendid hair.

But the question was always, how do we live now? What Jesus has done in the past—loved us, saved us, given us a future—stands behind us and in front of us. We were saved and we will be saved. But today we are not young believers or resurrected bodies. We are in the lumpy middle or the floppy end.

Richard's clear voice rang across the lawn. "By your resurrection you raised the dead and brought us from death to life."

I put my arm around Zach's shoulder, pulling his small frame closer as he burrowed deeper into my coat and felt the same surge of absurd wonder that I experience every time I see Richard. He's a resurrection preview. He lived to finish more massive books, play with his grandkids, and even record some of his own music. A surprising third act.

Time really is a circle; I can see that now. We are trapped between a past we can't return to and a future that is uncertain. And it takes guts to live here, in the hard space between anticipation and realization. How quickly we believe that nothing can be new again but then, look. Another Leonard Cohen song is being sung. *Hallelujah*.

The sermon was ready to begin. But as Richard opened his mouth to preach, he paused for a breath to glance back toward the gleaming tree line. His mouth twisted in a look of wry astonishment, as if surprised to see the sun rise once again.

WHEN THIS PANDEMIC IS finally over, I want to go back to a cathedral in the center of Portugal. I encountered it when my parents were on a lavish trip sailing around the world courtesy of a program called Semester at Sea, which allowed professors to teach students without a lot of learning involved. There were stops in South Africa and the Seychelles and Brazil, and my parents soaked in every cultural detail (cooking classes! camel riding! salsa dancing!) while students spent a great deal of time being briefed about the limits of alcohol consumption in each port. Toban and I decided to visit when the boat docked in Lisbon, Portugal, so we could celebrate another anniversary.

We took a day trip inland to see one of the great feats of Portuguese Catholic architecture, the towering Batalha Monastery. I headed out alone to explore its long stone corridors, pausing in its sumptuous courtyard before approaching the main sanctuary.

I noticed my dad up ahead as he strode through the massive archway. He turned around to stare at it appraisingly from the other side, his arms folded across his chest. I moved to stand beside him, gazing upward so I could soak it all in.

"Horrible, isn't it?" he mused, and we both burst out laughing.

"Are those . . . pineapples?" I asked, looking at the archway more closely. Indeed, they were. Hundreds of stone pineapples. And stone faces and stone flowers and stone lattices draped like webbing between each column lining the walls. Thousands upon thousands of tiny sculptures crowded every square inch of stone.

"Yes indeed. Late Gothic architecture is universally known to be the high water mark for adding doodly-dads to everything, but then the Portuguese managed to add *even more*." He shook his head with joyful disgust. The Portuguese fleets had brought back spoils from the New World and built splendid churches on the profits of the spice trade, and soon the altars of Lisbon were gilded so heavily that the marble floors had to be reinforced to support the weight of that much gold.

"It looks like there was an explosion," I concurred after some thought. "Let's just see what else the Portuguese can ruin, shall we?" I said, sweeping him into the next chapel.

Here the yellowed stone formed a massive octagonal chapel, each side vaulted and spectacularly ornamented. It was fussy and beautiful and ridiculous.

"Oh, it's perfect," muttered a voice nearby. It was an elderly man, binoculars flapping around his neck and white socks pulled high on his calves. He paced excitedly, glancing up and around on each side of the room "Ohhhhh, it is absolutely *perfect*."

I crossed the room slowly, trying to make out the pattern on the floor when I saw a massive shadow snake by. Alarmed, I looked up. A cloud passed overhead.

"Is this . . ."

"It was never finished, dear." The old man was smiling at me. "Isn't it wonderful?"

He gestured up, and where the ceiling should have been, there was only open sky. Seven kings had overseen the rise of this monument and had buried their dynasty in its walls. Yet none lived to finish it.

"The story goes that the plans for the building became so drawn out that eventually the idea of finishing it was simply abandoned. But it's much better this way," concluded the man, keeping pace beside me now as if we were old friends.

"What do you mean?" I asked.

"Don't you see? It's us! I can't imagine a more perfect expression of this life." He beamed at me. "I came all this way to see it. We're never done, dear. Even when we're done, we're never done."

He seemed a bit winded after this excitement, so we paused for a long moment so he could lean his narrow frame against one of the pineapple pillars. My father sauntered up to join us, and before he could announce his grand displeasure I chimed in quickly.

"Dad, my new friend here was telling me what he appreciates about this chapel."

"It's a masterpiece," affirmed the man, pulling his hat off of his white head and mopping his brow with a handkerchief he dug out of his pocket.

We gazed around for a long minute in silence.

The sun was beating down on us now and the man was beginning to look a bit fatigued by all this standing. We offered to walk him out, pausing at a few benches along the way. "Well, that was thrilling," he said at our departure, tipping his hat as he left us.

"I've been thinking," I said slowly, but my father was already there.

"Yes," he agreed, fixing the cathedral with a final stare. "It's wonderfully unnecessary, isn't it?"

All of our masterpieces, ridiculous. All of our striving, unnecessary. All of our work, unfinished, unfinishable. We do too much, never enough, and are done before we've even started.

It's better this way.

ACKNOWLEDGMENTS

·········

FINITUDE IS HARDEST ON THE PEOPLE WE love, and unfortunately I love a lot of people. So these are the heroes: Toban and Zach, thank you for carbonating our home with joy. Love you always. Karen, Gerry, Amy, and Maria, you are my chuthers. My Penners, my tribe, thank you for giving me a place to belong. Carolyn, Kori, Luke, Will, Stephen, Laceye, Thea, Leah, Sarah McHale, you prayed me through.

The ability to work throughout this illness made my life not simply bearable, but beautiful. Thank you to my mighty team at the Everything Happens Project at Duke Divinity School. Jessica Richie, you make every single day better. I could not have done any of this without you. Harriet Putman, we were never complete without you. Dave Odom, A.J. Walton, and Sara Hohnstein, your gifts make this sing. And to the guests of the Everything Happens podcast, you were the best weekly thing to happen to me.

Hilary Redmon and Christy Fletcher, you always believed. You have made me so much better than I am. Thank you to the Random House team for taking a chance on a very sick and sad professor. And a special thank you to Joel, whose yelling is the closest experience I will ever have to self-esteem. I would have added you to the dedication but I knew you'd be a dick about it.

APPENDIX

———

Clichés We Hear
and Truths We Need

Things People Say	A More Complicated Truth
Make a bucket list.	A life is never finished, even when it's over.
Carpe diem!	I mean, yes, unless you need a nap.
Everything happens for a reason.	We must learn to face uncertainty with courage.
Let go and let God.	God loves you, but won't do your taxes.

Things People Say	A More Complicated Truth
Be present.	We toggle between the past, present, and future for good reasons.
No regrets.	Facing the past is part of facing the future.
Make every minute count.	Life is unpredictable. You're a person, not a certified accountant.
Everyone is doing their best.	The jury is still out on that.
Nothing is wasted.	We lose every day. Which is why we will never have enough endless love, friends, and carbs.
Everything is possible.	Ask instead, what is possible today?
You are invincible.	There's no cure for being human.

KATE BOWLER is an associate professor of the history of Christianity in North America at Duke Divinity School. She completed her undergraduate degree at Macalester College, received a master's degree in religion from Yale Divinity School, and earned a PhD at Duke University. She is the author of the *New York Times* bestsellers *Everything Happens for a Reason* and *Good Enough* as well as *Blessed: A History of the American Prosperity Gospel* and *The Preacher's Wife: The Precarious Power of Evangelical Women Celebrities*. On her popular podcast, *Everything Happens*, she talks with people about what they have learned in difficult times and why it is so hard to speak frankly about suffering. She has appeared on the TED stage, NPR, and *Today*, and her writing has been featured in *The New York Times*, *The Washington Post*, and *Time*. She lives in Durham, North Carolina, with her husband, Toban, and son, Zach.

KateBowler.com
Facebook.com/KateCBowler
Twitter: @KateCBowler
Instagram: @katecbowler